River
Notes

Wade Davis

REVISED EDITION

A NATURAL AND HUMAN
HISTORY OF THE COLORADO

River
Notes

Drought and the Twilight
of the American West

DAVID SUZUKI INSTITUTE

 GREYSTONE BOOKS

Vancouver/Berkeley/London

Greystone Books Ltd.
greystonebooks.com

David Suzuki Institute
www.davidsuzukiinstitute.org

Cataloguing data available from Library and Archives Canada

ISBN 978-1-77840-142-8 (pbk.)
ISBN 978-1-77840-143-5 (epub)

Printed and bound in Canada on FSC® certified paper at Friesens. The FSC® label means that materials used for the product have been responsibly sourced.

Greystone Books thanks the Canada Council for the Arts, the British Columbia Arts Council, the Province of British Columbia through the Book Publishing Tax Credit, and the Government of Canada for supporting our publishing activities.

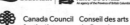

MIX
Paper from
responsible sources
FSC
www.fsc.org   FSC® C016245

Canadä

BRITISH COLUMBIA

BRITISH COLUMBIA
ARTS COUNCIL
An agency of the Province of British Columbia

Canada Council
for the Arts

Conseil des arts
du Canada

Greystone Books gratefully acknowledges the xʷməθkʷəy̓əm (Musqueam), Sḵwx̱wú7mesh (Squamish), and səlilwətaɬ (Tsleil-Waututh) peoples on whose land our Vancouver head office is located.

Contents

Man always kills the thing he loves.
And so we the pioneers have killed our wilderness.
Some say we had to. Be that as it may,
I am glad I shall never be young without
wild country to be young in.
Of what avail are forty freedoms without
a blank spot on the map?

—Aldo Leopold,
A Sand County Almanac, 1949

Introduction

The Grand Canyon is a story of time, the origins of the planet as revealed in rock and stone, but also the whirlwind of fortunes that can transform our destiny in a single generation.

I first visited the Grand Canyon in 1967 with two school friends and an elderly teacher who filled his summers by taking young students on long road trips, camping across the country. I mostly remember the color of the sky and the immensity of the chasm, with the Colorado River as seen from the canyon rim just a dirt thread lying across the bottom of the world. The nearest we got to the river was a mule ride down the Bright Angel Trail, three hours that left us sunburnt and swarming with ticks. Of the greater forces at play that summer, we were as oblivious as our teacher.

In retrospect, 1967 was an auspicious year for the army of engineers, planners, and developers whose confidence in their ability to tame the Colorado, transform the desert, and reimagine the hydrology of the American West had taken on a religious dimension, secured as if an article of faith.

The Glen Canyon Dam, built over a decade, had been formally dedicated by the president's wife, Lady Bird Johnson, on September 22, 1966. In scale, it was an astonishing feat of construction, a concrete arch surpassed in height only by its elegant sibling downstream, the Hoover Dam, an art deco masterpiece of engineering completed in 1935. Lake Mead above the Hoover Dam would remain the largest reservoir in the United States, but as the waters of the Colorado began to spread across the catchment of the Glen Canyon Dam in the first months of 1963, a vision emerged of a body of blue water in volume only slightly smaller than Lake Mead, but in scale and aspect incomparably more beautiful and dramatic.

To Floyd Dominy, the man ultimately responsible for the building of the Glen Canyon Dam—and its greatest champion—the reservoir that became Lake Powell was a thing of pure beauty, a miracle in the desert. "There is a natural order in our universe," Dominy famously wrote. "God created both Nature and Man. Man serves God, but Nature serves Man. To have a deep blue lake, where no lake was before, seems to bring Man a little closer to God."

Even his archrival, David Brower of the Sierra Club, haunted all his life by the loss of Glen Canyon, agreed that Dominy was a good man, even a great American, though very much a product of his times. Like so many of his generation, including my own father, Dominy believed that any natural resource not used was wealth wasted. He had been raised as a boy on a dying farm in Nebraska during the Dust Bowl. His first job as county agent in rural Wyoming was helping ranchers build earthen dams to secure water for their livestock. By his own account, he became a crusader for the development of water. As Commissioner of the Bureau of Reclamation, singularly responsible for water policy in the American West, Dominy was not just an advocate of massive water projects, dams, and canals designed to tame every river and divert water to the cities, farms, and settlements of the desert southwest; he was, in his own words, "the messiah."

As Lake Powell slowly came into being, with the flow of the Colorado shut down as if by a tap, there was little concern for the downstream consequences. In later years, conservation would sometimes trump engineering, but in 1963 ecological considerations hardly entered the conversation. The environmental movement was embryonic; as an organized political force it would only emerge in the wake of the dam's construction, catalyzed by the outrage provoked as the reservoir above the dam deepened and spread, flooding Glen Canyon, famously eulogized by photographer Eliot Porter as "the place no one knew."

The overwhelming national consensus in 1967 called for growth. Albuquerque's population had doubled in a decade. Las Vegas that year had a population of 181,000; Tucson, 274,000; Phoenix, 763,000. Each of these cities would grow at least five-fold in a generation, with Las Vegas increasing to 2.8 million, and Phoenix by 2022 achieving a population of 4.6 million. If few in 1967 anticipated such figures, it was evident to all, as Dominy never ceased to say, that if there was to be any growth at all, it would be dependent on water, stored in Lake Powell.

Thus, over twenty years, as the reservoir expanded, reaching in 1983 a maximum depth of 583 feet, extending in length 186 miles, with a width of 25 miles and 1,900 miles of shoreline, Lake Powell—celebrated as a recreational wonderland—became a symbol of human triumph, capacity, and resolve. It stored 20 million acre-feet of water—enough to fill 10 million Olympic-sized swimming pools—a vital repository that made possible the transformation of desert lands that would, in time, be home to 40 million Americans.

In 1973, construction began on the Central Arizona Project, a 336-mile diversion canal conceived to bring water from the Colorado—456 billion gallons altogether—to Phoenix and Tucson, even while providing irrigation for more than a million acres, allowing farmers to grow cotton, hay, and alfalfa in the desert. To secure federal funds to cover construction costs, Arizona cut a deal with California that was certain to haunt the state should the flow of the Colorado ever be compromised or reduced. But with water in abundance, there was little concern. That the open canal lost over five billion gallons of water each year to evaporation, and another three billion to leakage, was considered tolerable wastage, given the scale and benefits of the project.

As Lake Powell reached its maximum capacity in 1980, water levels five times what they are today, the future seemed exceedingly bright. The only threat to the dam came in 1983 when a surge of snowmelt into the reservoir raised lake levels to a dangerous extent, forcing the engineers to open the spillways for the first time since the initial construction. Abundance of water, not a shortage, marked the 1980s, a decade now recognized as having been unusually wet.

Floyd Dominy turned ninety in 2000, his faith in the transformative power of engineering unshaken, his dreams of greening the desert still vital and alive. But with the turning of the millennium, the weather changed, along with, as we now recognize, the climate. By the time he passed away a decade later, the entire basin of the Colorado was in the midst of a drought seemingly without end, the most severe to have struck the American Southwest in twelve hundred years.

CERTAINLY BY 2006, the signs were there. Indeed, it was growing concern about the state of the Colorado River, and a looming water crisis throughout the West, that drew me back to the Grand Canyon that year and ultimately led to the writing of *River Notes: A Natural and Human History of the Colorado*. It began, innocently enough, as a great adventure: an IMAX 3D film that brought cast and crew, photographers, models, sponsored athletes, and a host of bewildered river guides to the north bank of the Colorado at Lees Ferry on a hot summer's day not soon to be forgotten. With five motorized launches to carry several tons of equipment and supplies, three wooden dories, a half-dozen eighteen-foot whitewater rafts, and kayaks galore, we were less a river trip than a floating carnival, the largest flotilla ever granted a permit by the National Park to run the river.

The film project originated with Greg MacGillivray, a dedicated conservationist, and a legend in the world of IMAX. As both a pioneer and artistic master of the genre, with thirty-five IMAX films to his credit as director and cinematographer, Greg has a rare understanding of the emotional impact that large-format films, projected in perfect resolution on screens eighty feet tall, can have on an audience. Altogether, his films have grossed over $1 billion in ticket sales, an achievement without precedent for a documentary filmmaker. Commercial success fuels Greg's mission as a storyteller, and at the heart of his every story is love for the natural world, a passion that invariably leads him, a Californian surfer from childhood, back to water.

Having made a series of highly successful films about ocean conservation—*The Living Sea, Dolphins, Coral Reef Adventure*—Greg wanted to address the global freshwater crisis against the backdrop of the Colorado, at once the most iconic and compromised river in the United States. He envisioned a journey in which two fathers, each in their own ways advocates for the wild, would run the river with their daughters, just before the young women left home to attend university, each beginning her own journey in life.

With this premise in mind, Greg recruited me and my daughter Tara, along with my old college friend Bobby Kennedy Jr. and his daughter Kick. Tara and Kick, both sixteen, bonded from the start. Bobby and I could have been born in the same Irish crib. With Greg's crew, and so many inspired characters, shooting the film made for weeks of fun. Though there was much talk of the crisis— the falling levels of Lake Powell, the plight of the river delta, water issues throughout the American West—the

mood in camp and on the river remained invariably buoyant. At dawn, and beneath the spacious silence of the
night sky, gathered with friends, all sleeping in the sand,
the splendor of the river has a way of putting even the
most earnest of human concerns in perspective. The Colorado and its canyon will endure. This was Greg's message: "Deep in the canyon, where all is still, hope abounds."

Released in 2008, *Grand Canyon Adventure,* with a
soundtrack by the Dave Matthews Band, was a solid
success, generating some $31 million at the box office. To
accompany the film, we published an illustrated book,
Grand Canyon: River at Risk. Both in prepping for the
film and doing research for the book, I'd been surprised
to learn how few works of literary nonfiction, at least at
the time, addressed the complete saga of the Colorado
and the Grand Canyon. There were scores of photography books, no shortage of guidebooks, any number of
personal memoirs, and reams of technical publications on
geology, wildlife, the water crisis, and climate change. But
aside from the journals of John Wesley Powell, which few
manage to read, and Wallace Stegner's classic, *Beyond the
Hundredth Meridian,* there were only a handful of popular
books that took on the whole story.

With *River Notes,* I had in mind from the start a small
book, one you could readily pop in your backpack or river
bag. A text that would explain what you were seeing and
provide a context for what you were hearing from the
guides. The entire geological history of the canyon, for
example, condensed in eight pages, presented in a manner that made sense and could be readily understood. All

these wonderful themes: the mystery of the Anasazi; the power of the Mormon dream of Zion; the lost voices of the Zuni, Hopi, Havasupai, and Paiute; the prophetic passions of John Wesley Powell; the poetic ravings of Ed Abbey; the astonishing engineering achievements of the dam builders. *River Notes* was most assuredly not written as a work of environmental activism. It was simply the book that I wanted to have when going down the Colorado through the canyon, trying, and often failing, to make sense out of everything.

River Notes was published in 2012, four years after the launch of *Grand Canyon Adventure*. The book, though well received, met some unexpected resistance, as had the film. Just as a few IMAX venues worried about the film's focus on water issues, a number of commercial rafting companies were reluctant to recommend or stock the book out of concern that it might offend their wealthy clients. I found this both curious and slightly mystifying. Every guide I'd met on the Colorado was deeply and sincerely concerned about the plight of the river; George Wendt, founder of O.A.R.S. and the godfather of the entire commercial rafting scene on the Colorado, was with us during the film shoot. Conservation was all he and the young guides spoke about. In a generous endorsement, George described *River Notes* as "the perfect primer for Grand Canyon river guides, passengers, and armchair adventurers." He captured both the essence of the book and the reason I wrote it.

By any measure, the conservation messages of both the film and the book were mild; some might say tepid. When an initial edit of *Grand Canyon Adventure* was shown to test audiences, as is the norm with IMAX productions that play in family-friendly venues, often for months if not years, the survey results revealed an overwhelming demand for a much stronger conservation message. In response, Greg reconfigured the film, and we returned at considerable expense for an additional season of filming. The only overt environmental statement comes at the end of the film, as the credits roll over a series of short scenes of Kick and Tara encouraging everyone to reduce their domestic water use when taking showers, washing cars, or watering the grass. A gentle reminder, nothing more.

What made *River Notes* uncomfortable for some is precisely what gives the re-issue of the book relevance today—not because things have changed, but because so much has stayed the same. In 2006, the situation was ominous, but even the most vocal activists and conservationists found reassurance in knowing that the crisis they so earnestly anticipated still lay in the future, a long way off. Drought was acknowledged, but few believed it would extend for a generation and still be with us in 2023, its consequences rendered all the more severe by climate change. One could bemoan the plight of the river, criticize the profligate, herald environmental apocalypse while anticipating catastrophe by the campfire, without ever having to confront the fundamentals, the economic foundations, the very infrastructure of the world that Floyd Dominy had brought into being, and upon which everyone in the American Southwest—river guides included—now depended.

River Notes posed a challenge because in telling the story of the Colorado, the book exposed contradictions and structural flaws, if you will, in the foundational myths that have driven and sustained the entire settlement of the American West, from the hejira of the Mormons to the diversions that drain the last of the Colorado, allowing nothing of the river to reach the sea.

Not that I set out to do this, as if writing an exposé. I knew very little about anything that appears in *River Notes* until I experienced the river and researched the book. As much as anyone, I found it unsettling to learn that the entire water crisis in the American West comes down to cows eating alfalfa in a landscape where neither belongs. That the delta of the Colorado could be reborn with the water that today goes to produce a third of 1 percent of the nation's cattle production. That the federal government sets aside 250 million acres of open land for ranchers who produce less than 10 percent of America's beef. That no amount of water conservation in the home, on the golf course, or in the swimming pools and fountains of Los Angeles and Las Vegas will make a difference as long as half of the country's water supply is used to fatten cattle.

After all the efforts of all the engineers, and all the billions spent, the many hundreds of dams erected, the excavation of miles upon miles of canals and aqueducts, the total area brought into cultivation is roughly the size of Missouri—most of which was made arable by tapping a finite supply of groundwater. The wild rivers have everywhere been sacrificed, but the desert still rules the

American West. Without malice, and certainly without glee, *River Notes* suggested, if gently, that Floyd Dominy's world was crumbling, his dream dying, and with it our collective vision of Zion, imposed with undaunted courage and tenacity by generations of Americans upon a land that even God could not tame.

Americans don't do austere, as I quipped in *River Notes*, and to their credit they don't know the meaning of failure. Our reluctance to accept defeat, or adapt to a new reality, is evident in the choices we've made in the years since 2012. Growth remains the mantra. The cities of Arizona, Nevada, Utah, and California rank as the fastest-growing places in the country. Phoenix has increased in population faster than any American city. River water from the Colorado supports 15 million more people today than it did when Bill Clinton was elected president in 1992. Ten million more than it did in 2006, when we gathered to make our film. The river now serves one in ten Americans.

In *River Notes*, I wrote that the reservoirs of Lake Mead and Lake Powell were down to two-thirds capacity and might never again be full. With the drought then in its twelfth year, I cited climate models suggesting that it might be here to stay. We are today in the third decade of a drought that, despite heavy snowpacks in California and parts of the mountain west, remains unrelenting.

Over the last century, the river's flow has averaged roughly 15 million acre-feet a year, far less than the 17.5 million acre-feet that planners anticipated when water rights were apportioned to the seven states of the basin—Wyoming, Colorado, Utah, New Mexico, Nevada,

Arizona, and California—in 1922. In that year, the population of Arizona was roughly 350,000, that of Nevada a mere 80,000. Between 2000 and 2022, the flow of the river dropped to an average of 12 million acre-feet; over the last three years the annual flow has been but 10 million acre-feet. Even as the volume of water coming down the Colorado has dramatically declined, the seven states of the basin continue to clamor for allotments based on flawed assessments established nearly a century ago, exerting rights to consume what the river cannot provide.

As a result, during a drought of historic severity, water consumption has consistently surpassed the total natural flow of the river; altogether since 2000, water use has outstripped supply by 33.6-million acre-feet (an acre-foot is 325,851 gallons). To meet demand, water has been diverted from the major reservoirs. Lake Mead, last full in 1983, is today down to 28 percent of capacity, 1,040 feet above sea level, the lowest it has been since the floodgates closed in the 1930s. If the reservoir drops below 950 feet, the Hoover Dam will no longer generate hydroelectric power. At 895 feet, the reservoir becomes a deadpool; water can no longer pass through the dam. The river downstream ceases to exist.

The situation at Lake Powell is equally grim. Its capacity is now down to 22 percent. In February 2023, the reservoir dropped to 3,522 feet above sea level, the lowest since the Glen Canyon Dam became operational in 1963. Should the water level drop another 32 feet, which can readily occur in a year, it will no longer be possible to generate electricity that today powers and cools the homes and businesses of 4.5 million citizens. A power outage in Phoenix, coinciding with a two-day heat wave, could result in half the population—800,000 or more—seeking emergency care in hospitals set up to handle but 3,000 patients. An estimated 12,800 would die. At 3,370 feet, Lake Powell will reach deadpool. The Glen Canyon Dam will be but a concrete plug. Water will cease to flow, cutting off the drinking supply of well over 25 million Americans, including most of those living in Phoenix, Las Vegas, Tucson, and much of the Los Angeles basin.

As Lake Powell recedes, yet another challenge emerges. The Colorado below the Glen Canyon Dam runs clear and cold, its heavy sediment load having settled in the reservoir above the dam. In the early years, the Bureau of Reclamation attempted to monitor these deposits, before giving up in the 1980s, confident that it would take, as was claimed, seven hundred years for Lake Powell to fill up. Asked about the dangers posed by the sediments, Floyd Dominy replied, "We will let people in the future worry about it."

The future unfortunately is now. The entire story of the Grand Canyon is one of wind, water, silt, and sand. Since the Glen Canyon Dam went up sixty years ago, the equivalent of sixty-one supersized Mississippi River bargeloads of sand and mud have been deposited in Lake Powell every day. The total accumulation would bury the length of Manhattan to a depth of 126 feet—close to the height of a twelve-storey building.

As the reservoir has shrunk, this silt, exposed to the sun, has formed what can best be described as mud glaciers. As lake levels fall, a gradient is formed, down which these massive sediment accretions are moving at a rate of a hundred feet or more per day toward the dam. Should they reach and plug the dam, threatening the integrity of the structure, the only option would be to bore tunnels at the base of the dam, allowing the sediments to pass, while killing for good the reservoir. "That natural sediment load," notes Jack Schmidt, director of the Center for Colorado River Studies at Utah State University, "cannot be blocked from the sea forever."

In the meantime, ordinary American families are already experiencing shortages that would have been unthinkable in 2006. For decades, the Arizona city of Scottsdale has provided the Rio Verde Foothills, a community of two thousand homes, with access to its municipal water supply, sourced from the Colorado. On January 1, 2023, this supply was cut, a decision made by a city facing its own crisis, leaving the people of Rio Verde no option but to buy water by the truckload at prices that tripled overnight. Those who dug wells discovered that, after years of drought, the water table had fallen by hundreds of feet. Residents have turned to using paper plates and urinating outside, even while coping with monthly water bills as costly as their mortgage payments.

Cities such as Las Vegas have implemented strict conservation measures, banning ornamental grass, limiting water deliveries to golf courses, reducing the size of swimming pools, using recycled water whenever possible. Yet despite these efforts, Las Vegas still uses twice as much water as the average US consumption. Hedging its bets, the city is building a three-mile-long tunnel that will come up at the bottom of Lake Mead, a $1.4-billion drain to ensure that if the reservoir ever runs dry, Las Vegas will get the last drop.

In the end, what Las Vegas and other cities do hardly matters, for the elephant in the room remains agriculture. Fully 80 percent of the water drawn from the Colorado goes to irrigating some 5.5 million acres, most of which is used to grow alfalfa and grass to feed cattle, and not only in the United States. Alfalfa grown in Arizona is exported by the ton to fatten cattle in Asia and the Middle East.

Even as the Bureau of Reclamation in 2014 issued reports warning of a looming freshwater crisis, Saudi Arabia's largest dairy company, Almarai, through its subsidiary Fondomonte, began buying and leasing land across western Arizona. In one agreement, as reported by *The Arizona Republic*, the state authority leased Almarai thirty-five hundred acres of public land at one sixth market value. In rural Arizona, groundwater is largely unregulated; whoever has the money can drill a well and lay claim to the water. Thus, as household wells were running dry with the falling water table, a Saudi agricultural giant was permitted to use deep industrial wells to extract unlimited amounts of groundwater, allowing it to grow alfalfa in one desert to feed dairy cows eight thousand miles away in another desert, in a water-stressed nation that has, for all the right reasons, banned the cultivation of the crop within its own borders.

Utah dedicates fully 68 percent of its available water to growing alfalfa, even though livestock generate an insignificant 0.2 percent of the state's income. In California, it takes 3.2 gallons of water to produce a single almond. Such grotesque inefficiencies would suggest an easy fix, if only the problem were so simple. If Americans eliminated meat from their diet for just one day each week, it would save a volume of water equivalent to the entire annual flow of the Colorado, which on paper would go a long way to alleviating the crisis. But it would also imply economic losses in the millions, with annual meat consumption nationwide dropping by over 10 billion pounds. In 2021, almonds ranked as California's top agricultural export, generating sales in excess of $4.7 billion.

Agriculture's claim to the Colorado is inviolable, if only because the irrigated fields of the basin provide so much of our food. California, the largest consumer, has rights to 3.1 million acre-feet—as much as Arizona and Nevada combined—in good measure because the state produces a third of the country's vegetables and three-quarters of our fruits and nuts. The Imperial Valley alone grows most of the country's broccoli and a good share of the lettuce, all made possible by the waters of the Colorado. As Californians see it, they feed the nation, while their rival states upriver—Arizona and Nevada—cultivate urban sprawl, which places ever more pressure on a diminishing supply of water upon which everyone's survival depends. In other words, it's California farms versus subdivisions in Las Vegas. Avocados and almonds taking on the challenge of the wealth generated by the fastest-growing cities in the country.

Negotiations between California, Nevada, and Arizona are especially fraught, as they are the states most dependent on water from the large reservoirs, Lake Mead and Lake Powell, and they alone can be forced by the federal government to reduce consumption. In August 2021, as water levels in Lake Mead reached new lows, Washington finally decided to act. Invoking the impact of the historic drought, the Department of the Interior formally declared an emergency water shortage on the Colorado, an unprecedented move that triggered immediate reductions in water deliveries to certain states—including Arizona, which lost fully a fifth of its allocation. Altogether, the seven states of the original 1922 Colorado River Compact—again Wyoming, Colorado, Utah, New Mexico, Nevada, Arizona, and California—were ordered to reduce their consumption by four million acre-feet, as much as 30 percent of the total flow of the river.

Six of the states agreed on a plan, but California—the greatest consumer—held out, citing its agreement with Arizona, which had allowed the construction of the Central Arizona Project back in 1973. California proposed that its share be reduced by 17 percent, while Arizona's be cut in half. If implemented, California's 800-square-mile Imperial Valley would receive more water from Lake Mead than the entire state of Arizona; the flow in the aqueduct that brings drinking water to Phoenix and Tucson would be reduced to a trickle.

At an impasse, the states did nothing. A year went by before the Bureau of Reclamation took them to task, demanding a plan of action. California once again targeted Arizona; the six other states went after California. In the absence of any agreement, the next step appeared to be litigation. The last time California and Arizona went to court to fight over water rights, the case consumed eleven years. Should a new legal battle drag on, with Lake Mead and Lake Powell falling every month nearer to deadpool, the lawyers may just find themselves, as former Secretary of the Interior Bruce Babbitt notes in a recent editorial, fighting over a wasteland.

On April 11, 2023, the Biden administration set in motion at least the beginnings of a solution to the immediate crisis. An environmental review issued that day by the Department of the Interior began with the obvious. The nation could either prioritize the farmers of California based on water allocations determined a century ago and utterly anachronistic today, or it could spread the pain across all states and all Americans affected by the crisis. A third option was to do nothing, which was clearly unacceptable.

The importance of this federal review lay less in what it said than in what it implied. While acknowledging that the seven states of the basin retain certain rights encoded in law and exercised by tradition, the Department of the Interior affirmed its own authority to determine how, when, and for what "beneficial use" water could be released from the reservoirs. The message was clear. Washington had the legal tools to intervene. With Secretary of the Interior Deb Haaland having set a deadline for August 2023 for the states to come to some kind of agreement, California, in particular, came under immediate pressure to compromise. On the eve of the 2024 presidential election, with Arizona, Nevada, and New Mexico critical to Democratic prospects, the Biden administration was not about to let Phoenix and Tucson, not to mention Las Vegas, run dry.

Placing the fate of the Colorado above the rights of states, in a manner without precedent in American history, President Biden was clearly ready to impose, if necessary, unilateral reductions that would see water deliveries to California, Arizona, and Nevada reduced evenly by as much as 25 percent. A decade ago, such a declaration might well have prompted a legal challenge from the states. Today, with reservoirs running dry, a protracted legal battle is in the interests of no one — not the people, and certainly not the river.

Instead, the parties came up with a temporary solution. In a compromise announced on May 22, 2023, the federal government pledged $1.2 billion to irrigation districts, cities, and Native American tribes throughout the lower Colorado Basin in exchange for a commitment to voluntarily reduce water consumption by a total of 2.3 million acre-feet. An additional reduction of 700,000 acre-feet will come from California, Arizona, and Nevada, in a manner to be determined by them. Should the three states fail to reach an accord, the Bureau of Reclamation is empowered to withhold the entire allotment.

If fully implemented, consumption will be reduced across the lower basin by three million acre-feet, roughly

13 percent of the water currently used. It's not enough, but it is a beginning. If formally adopted by Congress, and extended beyond its current expiry date in 2026, this agreement will be good for the cities of Arizona and Nevada, as well as the thirty Native American tribes that have their own rights to the river. Perhaps not so great in the short term for some farmers in California. But certainly, in the end, it will be a blessing for all Americans, especially those whose lives have been touched by the river.

The Colorado River is the story of the American West, and the West is the story of America. In the early years of settlement, those who endured unimaginable hardships to build a life in the desert saw their mission as a mandate from God. That conviction drove them to survive. Today, along the drought-scorched borderlands, where the river defines the frontier with Mexico, in churches of adobe and cane, evangelical pastors call on the same God as they preach a gospel of salvation for the river, which they herald as a gift from the divine.

At Iglesia Betania, a small Pentecostal church in Yuma, Arizona, in a trailer park half a mile from the Mexican border, the congregation prays for the Colorado at every service. Their pastor, Reverend Victor Venalonzo, reminds them that of the four rivers mentioned in the Book of Genesis, only two, the Tigris and Euphrates, still exist. From the pulpit, Reverend Venalonzo describes the Colorado as the lifeblood of the people. As he told Fernanda Santos, reporting for the *New York Times*, he used to hold baptisms along its shores, until the river became so shallow that even children had to sit on the bottom to be fully immersed in the water. Now he must hold the ceremonies in the church. The riverbed is dry. He worries that his granddaughter will grow up knowing only that there was once a river running through their lives. For this reason, he prays for the Colorado.

I can't confirm that the reverend's prayers have been answered, but good news has at last brightened the prospects of the Colorado. Across the upper basin of the river, in the mountains of New Mexico, Utah, Colorado, and Wyoming, the record snowfalls during the winter of 2022–23 have begun to melt. Those monitoring the reservoirs report that the volume of spring runoff flowing into both Lake Mead and Lake Powell is one-and-a-half times larger than normal. In Utah, the Great Salt Lake, which has lost almost two thirds of its volume since 1985 (including forty billion gallons of water annually since 2000), has been replenished with a flood of snowmelt. That meltwater has raised the lake's level three feet above where it stood in November 2022, when it reached a record low of just 37 percent of its former volume. At its lowest point, there was real concern that the lake would be completely gone within five years. Now, it has a new chance. A season of snow does not imply that the crisis is past, or even that the drought has ended. But perhaps it will provide a reprieve, allowing us time to make the difficult decisions and implement the measures that the crisis has long demanded.

Between AD 1275 and 1300, the Anasazi, a civilization that had thrived in the canyonlands for a thousand years, simply vanished, abandoning their urban centers, their irrigated lands, their sacred enclosures. Their descendants, the Hopi and Zuni, tell of a time of drought, the end of the rains. Without food in the desert, one can live for a fortnight; without water, perhaps a day. The collapse of the Anasazi occurred in a single generation. The drought in the American Southwest has now entered its twenty-third year. *River Notes* asks only that we take this to heart, even as we celebrate a river that in so many ways has made us who we are.

River
Notes

~

In 1922, having completed work on the first comprehensive management plan for the Grand Canyon, Aldo Leopold, along with his younger brother, set out by canoe to explore the mouth of the mighty Colorado. At the time the main flow of the Colorado reached the sea, carrying with it each year millions of tons of silt and sand and so much fresh water that the river's influence extended some forty miles into the Gulf of California. The alluvial fan of the delta spread across two million acres, well over three thousand square miles, a vast riparian and tidal wetland the size of the state of Rhode Island. It was one of the largest desert estuaries on earth. Off shore, nutrients brought down by the river supported an astonishingly rich fishery for *bagre* and *corvina*, dolphins, and the rare and elusive vaquita porpoise, the world's smallest marine cetacean. At the top of the food chain was the *totoaba*, an enormous relative of the white sea bass that grew to three hundred pounds, spawned in the brackish waters of the estuary and swarmed in the Sea of Cortez in such abundance that even fishermen blinded in old age, it was said, had no difficulty striking home their harpoons.

In contrast to the searing sands of the Sonoran Desert through which the lower Colorado flowed, and the blue and barren hills of the Sierra de los Cucapás, cradling the river valley to the north and west, the delta was lush and fertile, a "milk and honey wilderness," as Leopold called it, of marshes and emerald ponds with cattails and wild grasses yielding to the wind, and cottonwoods, willows, and mesquite trees overhanging channels where the water ran everywhere and nowhere, as if incapable of settling upon a route to the sea. The river, wrote Leopold, "could not decide which of a hundred green lagoons offered the most pleasant and least speedy path to the gulf. So he travelled them all, and so did we. He divided and rejoined, he twisted and turned, he meandered in awesome jungles, he all but ran in circles, he dallied with lovely groves, he got lost and was glad of it, and so were we."

Drifting with the ebb and flow of the tides, waking by dawn to the whistles of quail roosting in the branches of mesquite trees, making camp on mudflats etched with the tracks of wild boar, yellowlegs, and jaguar, the Leopold brothers experienced the Colorado delta much as had the Spanish explorer Hernando de Alarcón, who first reached its shores in 1540. There were bobcats draped over cottonwood snags. Deer, raccoons, beavers, and coyotes, and flocks of birds so abundant they darkened the sky. Avocets and willets, mallards, widgeons, and teals, scores of cormorants, screaming gulls, and so many egrets on the wing that Leopold compared them in flight to "a premature snowstorm." He wrote of great phalanxes of geese sideslipping toward the earth, falling like autumn leaves. On every shore he saw clapper rails and sandhill cranes, and overhead, doves and raptors scraping the sky.

It was an exquisite landscape, rich in fauna and flora, with hundreds of species of birds and rare fish, and along the mudflats, melons and wild grasses that yielded great handfuls of edible fruits and seeds. But the brothers' sojourn in the delta was not without its challenges. The river was too muddy to drink, the lagoons too brackish, and every night they had to dig to find potable water. The dense and impenetrable thickets of *cachinilla* made movement on land almost impossible, leaving Leopold doubtful that people had ever lived in the wetlands. "The Delta having no place names," he wrote, "we had to devise our own as we went."

In this Leopold was quite wrong, for the marshes and lagoons of the Colorado delta had for a thousand years been home to the Cocopah people, who viewed themselves as the offspring of mythical gods, twins who had emerged from beneath the primordial water to create the firmament, the earth, and every living creature. In 1540 Hernando de Alarcón encountered at the mouth of the river not hundreds but thousands of men and women, who, in their rituals, he reported, revealed a deep reverence for the sun. He described the Cocopah as tall and strong, with bodies and faces adorned in paint. The men wore loincloths, the women coverings of feathers that fell back and front from the waist. Every adult man had shell ornaments hanging from the nose and ears, and deer bones suspended from bands of cordage wrapped around the arms. They gathered in great numbers, small bands of a hundred, larger assemblies of a thousand, and in one instance, as Alarcón reported, no fewer than six thousand.

To support such populations, the Cocopah grew watermelons and pumpkins, corn, beans, and squash. From

the wild they feasted on fish, wood rats, beavers, raccoons, feral dogs, and cattail pollen and tule roots. In the
first months of the year, with their stores of harvested
food exhausted, they travelled to the high desert to gather
cactus and agave. Mesquite pods, ground with a *metate*,
yielded flour that was made into cakes or mixed with water and consumed as a drink. Their dwellings were simple
structures—round domes of reeds and brush. They slept
beneath blankets of rabbit skins. They moved through the
marshes in dugout canoes, carved from cottonwood, or
on rafts of logs bound together by ropes made from willow bark or wild grasses.

Their most elaborate rituals occurred at death. The
body of the deceased was fully adorned and then cre-
mated, along with all possessions and memories. Shelters
were burned and even footprints eradicated to ensure that
the spirits of the dead abandoned all attachments and
were never tempted to return to the realm of the living.
The destiny of the dead was a land of plenty, not far from
home—salt flats near the mouth of the river. At the funeral ceremony, the orator shaman recalled all the events
in the life of the departed, as the relatives danced, moving four times around the burning pyre, wailing, sobbing,
and singing the songs of death. With the body nearly
consumed, the women of the family turned their backs
to the flames and solemnly cut off their hair as a sign of
mourning. Then, with the healing smoke of tobacco and
the relief of a ritual bath, each severed all connection to
the deceased, even as wood in massive amounts was added

to the fire to create a light that would shine through the night and illuminate in every corner of the delta the pathways of the living.

Standing today on the banks of what was once a river, looking across a channel of white sand and past the scrub and scabrous vegetation that stretches across barren mudflats to the horizon, it is impossible to imagine a time when such funerary rituals could have occurred in the delta of the Colorado. As recently as the last years of the nineteenth century the wetlands produced enough wood to fuel the steamships and paddle wheelers that supplied all of the army outposts, mining camps, and ragtag settlements of the lower Colorado. Today the gallery forests of cottonwood and willow are a shadow of memory, displaced by thickets of tamarisk and arrowweed, invasive species capable of surviving in soils poisoned by salt. The emerald lagoons are long gone, as are the migratory birds that in the tens of thousands once found refuge in the wetlands. In the sea the *totoaba* were hunted to near extinction, four million pounds a year by the 1940s, with individual fish selling for as little as five cents, and many thousands killed only for their bladders, dried as a delicacy to be used in Chinese soups, while the carcasses were left to rot in the desert sun. Marine productivity has fallen by as much as 95 percent, and all that remains to recall the bounty of the estuary are the countless millions of shells that form the islands and beaches on the shore. These, along with the memories of Cocopah elders still living today who can recall swimming in the lagoons as children, and gathering wild grasses and hunting deer in the twilight with their families.

"Man always kills the thing he loves," wrote Aldo Leopold, as he recalled his time in the Colorado delta, "and so we the pioneers, have killed our wilderness." Within twenty years of his visit, most of the wildlife had disappeared. The fishery that had fed the people of the river for generations was severely diminished, and the Cocopah population had dropped to fewer than fifteen hundred.

Just before his death in 1948 Leopold famously articulated in *A Sand County Almanac* a new ethic of the land, one that might embrace "an intelligent humility toward man's place in nature" and a definition of community that would expand to include its natural capital, the water and soil, plants and animals, the very land itself.

"Do we not already sing our love for and obligation to the land of the free and the home of the brave?," he asked. "Yes, but just what and whom do we love? Certainly not the soil, which we are sending helter skelter down river. Certainly not the waters, which we assume have no func tion except to turn turbines, float barges, and carry off sewage. Certainly not the plants, of which we exterminate whole communities without batting an eye. Certainly not the animals, of which we have already extirpated many of the largest and most beautiful species. A land ethic of course cannot prevent the alteration, management, and use of these 'resources,' but it does affirm their right to continued existence, and, at least in spots, their continued existence in a natural state. In short, a land ethic changes the role of *Homo sapiens* from conqueror of the land-community to plain member and citizen of it. It implies respect for his fellow-members, and also respect for the community as such."

Unfortunately Leopold's message came both too soon and too late for the delta of the Colorado, the very landscape that had in good measure inspired it. With the completion of Hoover Dam in 1935, the flow of the Colorado was dramatically reduced for six years, as the engineers allowed the reservoir dubbed Lake Mead to reach its capacity. The ecological implications of turning off a river like a tap evidently were never considered, any more than they were some thirty years later when the river's flow was once again curtailed with the construction of Glen Canyon Dam, which shut down the river for seventeen years until Lake Powell reached its design threshold in 1980. Downstream from the reservoirs, the Colorado is fed by a number of tributaries, but these flows in turn were cut off by other diversions, such as the Imperial Dam and the Morelos Dam, which captures Mexico's entire allotment, the last 10 percent of the river's flow, bringing water to Tijuana and Mexicali and allowing farmers to grow alfalfa, cotton, and corn in a desert basin that receives less than three inches of rain a year.

What reaches the mudflats of the delta today is agricultural runoff, wastewater that has flowed over fields, seeped into desert soils high in mineral salts, and pooled in reservoirs and back channels exposed to the sun. What once was a majestic river that each year in flood flushed clean the delta, replenishing the land with silt and nutrients, is today a saline slurry, with a salt content so high it cannot be used to water even the most hardy of garden plants. Thus by the time water provided to ranchers and farmers in the upper Colorado basin for a mere $3.50 an acre-foot reaches the delta, it must be treated and desalinated before it can be placed on Mexican fields, increasing the costs a hundredfold.

To walk down a gravel road just south of the border town of San Luis Rio Colorado and watch what remains of the Colorado pass through rusted culverts, bringing not fertility but toxicity to the land, is to ask what on earth became of this stream so revered in the American imagination, and yet now so despoiled that it today reaches the ocean a river only in name.

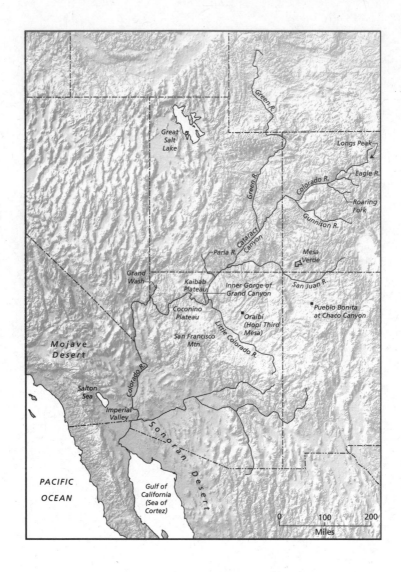

The grandeur of the Canyon confers
dignity on every form of life within its walls,
even down unto the meanest and the most petty.
It is an honor to be a visitor in the
Grand Canyon of the Colorado, as it is an honor
and a privilege to be alive, however briefly,
on this marvelous planet we call Earth.

—Edward Abbey, *One Life at a Time, Please*, 1988

God created both man and nature.
And man serves God, but nature serves man. . . .
To have a deep blue lake, where no lake was before,
seems to bring man a little closer to God.

—Floyd Dominy, Bureau of Reclamation commissioner,
Lake Powell: Jewel of the Colorado, 1965

Men may dam it and say that they have made a lake,
but it will still be a river. It will keep its nature and
bide its time, like a caged animal alert for the
slightest opening. In time, it will have its way;
the dam, like the ancient cliffs, will be carried away
piecemeal in the currents.

—Wendell Berry,
The Unforeseen Wilderness, 1991

~

A single fact of geography defines the American West. The clouds that sweep across the Pacific bring rain to the western flank of the Sierra Nevada and drop as much as 150 inches annually on the forests of the northern Cascades. From the east and south, weather patterns bring moisture from the Atlantic and the Gulf, ensuring that no land in the eastern half of the United States receives less than twenty inches of annual precipitation. But travel west of the 100th meridian, a line of longitude that bisects the Dakotas and Nebraska, running through Dodge City, Kansas, and the dusty back alleys and cattle pens of Abilene, Texas, and you will encounter no place in a thousand miles, from the Mexican frontier in the south to the Canadian border in the north, that receives more than twenty inches of rain in a year. Cities such as Phoenix, Las Vegas, El Paso, and Reno, home to millions, receive less than seven inches annually, as much rain as can fall in Mobile or Miami in a long afternoon.

The entire region, an area the size of Western Europe, was once known as the Great American Desert. But deserts are places of scarcity, minimalist landscapes that, however beautiful, are perceived as being innately hostile, austere, and infertile. Austerity is a notion foreign to the American ethos. Thus as the frontier moved west the nomenclature of place shifted and the desert was transformed in language if not in fact, becoming the Great Basin, the Colorado and Columbia Plateaus, the Snake River Plain, the Blue Mountains, and the Bitterroot

Range. But the stark reality remained. The Great Salt Lake, the Black Rock and Painted, the Great Sandy and Death Valley, the Mojave and the Sonoran are all deserts, as dry as many parts of the Sahara. The great cities and scattered towns, the ranches and grim farmsteads, the roadside strip malls, motels, and filling stations, the broken down drive-ins and every blue highway pawnshop and plywood souvenir trading post between Taos and Yuma could not exist without the massive manipulation of water.

To engineer this hydrological sleight of hand, there are only two sources and both are ephemeral. Beneath the ground are vast aquifers, remnants of the Ice Age, finite pools as precious and readily depleted as oil. On the surface, exposed to the relentless sun, are the wild rivers, running like serpents among the ancient rocks and mesas, their flows originating in the snow and ice fields of distant mountains. The largest in terms of volume is the Columbia, which rises in Canada, and its major tributary, the Snake, which is born near the headwaters of the Missouri in the heart of Yellowstone. The longest is the Rio Grande, which runs six hundred miles south from the San Juan Mountains of Colorado along the western flank of the Sangre de Cristo range, passing through Albuquerque to El Paso, where it turns east and for twelve hundred miles forms the international border before reaching the Gulf of Mexico and the Caribbean sea.

The third of the great rivers is the Colorado, smaller in volume than the Columbia, shorter than the Rio Grande, but surpassing both in its status as the American Nile, the river of the desert west, the muse of poets and song-writers, river guides, shamans, medicine women, eco-warriors, engineers, dam builders, and every farmer from the Grand Valley of Colorado to the Imperial Valley of California. Plugged by no fewer than twenty-five dams, the Colorado is the world's most regulated river drainage, providing most of the water supply for Las Vegas, Tucson, and San Diego, and much of the power and water for Los Angeles and Phoenix, five cities that are home to more than twenty-five million people. If the Colorado ceased flowing the water held in its multiple reservoirs might hold out for three to four years, but after that it would be necessary to abandon most of southern California and Arizona, and much of Colorado, New Mexico, Nevada, Utah, and Wyoming. For the entire American Southwest the Colorado is indeed the river of life, which makes it all the more tragic and ironic that by the time it approaches its final destination, it has been reduced to a shadow upon the sand, its delta dry and deserted, its flow a toxic trickle seeping into the sea.

~

No matter how far you have wandered hitherto,
or how many famous gorges and valleys you have seen,
this one, the Grand Cañon of the Colorado, will seem
as novel to you, as unearthly in the color and
grandeur and quantity of its architecture, as if you
have found it after death, on some other star.

—John Muir, *Our National Parks*, 1901

The Colorado is not now and never was a large river. In the Amazon, it would scarcely rank as a serious tributary. Dwarfed even within North America by the Missouri and Mississippi, the Yukon, Mackenzie, and St. Lawrence, it is remarkable less for its size than for its setting, the sandstone desert through which it flows. Born of the snowmelt on the west face of Longs Peak just beyond the Continental Divide in Rocky Mountain National Park, the river falls first into a small alpine lake at La Poudre Pass, and then begins a wild ride down the flank of the Cordillera, picking up the runoff of most of western Colorado. Joined by the Eagle and the Roaring Fork, it flattens its trajectory in the Grand Valley, picking up the Gunnison at Grand Junction, before moving west into Utah. Running south past Moab and Dead Horse Point, it fuses with the Green, its largest tributary, just above Cataract Canyon, and then flows southwest to be absorbed today, along with the San Juan, in a massive reservoir known as Lake Powell. Before the construction of Glen Canyon Dam, the river here ran free for 170 miles through a realm of magic, a canyon land so remote it could be destroyed without notice or attention, and yet so exquisite that its loss would be mourned for generations. The photographer Eliot Porter referred to Glen Canyon very simply as "the place no one knew."

What is remembered of Glen Canyon has been distilled from the notes and letters, the photographs and memories of the very few who had the privilege to experience its wonders, and to know the silence of the innumerable stars that once shone upon its depths. Most of what they say is that the river was unexpectedly calm, at least when not in flood. After its tumultuous descent from the snow and ice, a drop of several thousand feet in less than three hundred miles, the Colorado at Glen Canyon entered a place of color and shadow, where red undulating Navajo Sandstone cliffs enclosed a hidden realm where, in the words of a photographer who knew it well, the light itself had a physical, even sensual, presence. The deep blue of a spring sky, the emerald green of hanging gardens of ferns and mosses, the towering cliffs stained black by rainwater and runoff, the blue glow of moonlight, a thin crescent of night sky over white sandbars of willow and oak. In alcoves and seeps, bank beavers moved among the reeds, and deer browsed in the shade of redbud trees. One woke at dawn to the raucous sound of ravens and the singsong music of canyon wrens. And beneath every overhang, up every wash, in the shadow of cliffs on ground beyond reach of the seasonal floods were to be found not hundreds but thousands of Anasazi remains, ancient granaries and petroglyphs, stairways carved into stone, the remnant walls of house sites and kivas, the patterned outlines of irrigation ditches and channels, all of which disappeared beneath the rising waters when Glen Canyon Dam closed its flood gates in 1963.

The river running through Glen Canyon and past these exquisite ruins must have been a wild spectacle. Its flow ranged from a summer low of a few thousand cubic feet per second to a spring surge of more than three hundred thousand cubic feet per second, more than ten times the balanced stream artificially maintained today by the technicians at the spillways. When the summer monsoons broke and the draws and side canyons flashed in flood, these seasonal fluctuations might play out in a single day. The entire canyon would be swept clean to the high-water mark, with vast beaches and boulder fields, formidable rapids and willowy copses of vegetation simply swallowed in a gargantuan surge of water that was less a river than a slurry carrying an entire desert to the sea. Every year the wild Colorado drew some two hundred million tons of silt down its myriad of canyons. The average daily sediment load was five hundred thousand tons, enough to fill a hundred freight trains, each with a hundred cars, with each car bearing a load of two hundred thousand pounds.

Some of this desert dirt settled out in the calm and smooth stretches of the river above the major cataracts, forming each year new beaches and sandbars, which were soon colonized by scores of ephemeral plants, milkweeds and datura, bear grass and evening primroses. But much of the silt and sand flushed the length of the river, through Marble Canyon and Grand Canyon, coming to a rest only below the last of the great rapids, some two hundred miles from the Gulf of California, where the gradient finally leveled off and the river slowed. Here it built up, so dramatically that the riverbed itself would rise, year by year, as if the entire vast delta lay poised on a hydraulic lift. Inevitably and unpredictably the Colorado, constrained only by banks of silt, would break through and with the power of a flood forge new paths to the sea. Over the millennia these routes were revisited time and again, with some channels flowing south into what became Mexico, and others favoring a northerly course, away from the sea. There were times when gravity trumped geography and the river turned away from the ocean to disgorge to the north into a vast low basin of the Imperial Valley, where it formed an evanescent lake, the Salton Sea, today California's largest landlocked body of water. Then, as if an animate being, its whims satisfied, the river would within a few decades reverse its course and once again make its way for the sea, returning life to the delta.

As a result of these meanderings, Colorado River sediments became deposited over a vast area and to depths that promised enormous wealth to anyone who could learn to farm in the desert air. Yuma, Arizona, a historic river crossing just east of the California state line, is a hundred miles from the sea, but thanks to the accumulation of silt, it sits atop eighty feet of sediments which, if augmented by nitrogen and water, are transformed into some of the most fertile and productive soils in the United States. Statistically it is the sunniest place on the planet, and consistently the hottest city in the country, with summer temperatures averaging 117°F. Yuma receives a mere four inches of precipitation a year, and yet it is the lettuce capital of the world, producing 95 percent of the winter crop for all of North America. The water, of course, comes from the river, which means that nearly all of us, wherever we live in the country, drink from the Colorado, virtually half the days of our lives.

~

*Sired by the muddy Colorado in magnificent canyon
country, a great blue lake has been born in the West. . . .
Lake Powell holds working water—water for
many purposes. And one of those purposes is to provide
the people of this country with the finest scenic and
recreational area in the Nation.*

—Floyd Dominy, Bureau of Reclamation commissioner,
Lake Powell: Jewel of the Colorado, 1965

*In creating the lovely and the usable,
we have given up the incomparable.*

—Wallace Stegner, "Glen Canyon Submersis,"
The Glen Canyon Reader, 2003

In the early morning light the landing at Lees Ferry is
fired with activity as both private and commercial river
expeditions scramble to get their rafts rigged and their
clients ready to launch at the precise time allocated by the
permitting process. For all the easy camaraderie, there is
a palatable energy, a nervous excitement of anticipation
and foreboding that comes with the realization, especially
for the private parties, some of which have waited years
for the privilege, that the river passage of their dreams
is about to begin. The guides, weathered and sun beaten,
go about their tasks with an easy insouciance, while the
clients flutter about in sunhats and brightly colored long-
sleeved shirts, trying to be useful, pausing from time to
time to slather on another layer of sunscreen, all the while

chatting nervously about nothing in particular, as their eyes, hidden behind shades, dart back and forth between parking lot and the river. Rows of late model pickups overflow into a second lot, and a third. Some parties will travel only as far as Phantom Ranch, but most will go the distance to Diamond Creek, a fortnight's journey of 226 miles. No one travels light, and the steady stream of gear and food boxes moving toward the shore suggests a commando operation, fully equipped and a bit excessive.

As a private party of dories sets off, heading down toward the mouth of the Paria River and into Marble Canyon, large motorized snout boats land at the dock from upriver, disgorging thirty and forty passengers at a time, families for the most part, who have enjoyed a four-hour outing from a landing beneath the vaulted arch of Glen Canyon Dam. Children scamper toward the rafts and stare in wonder at the guides while their parents walk slowly uphill over the asphalt toward the waiting buses. A long queue forms outside the public toilets.

There are fly fishermen on the shore awaiting launches that will carry them upstream where, in cool clear waters in the shadow of dense thickets of tamarisk, they will flog the back eddies and pools of what has become one of the premier trophy trout fisheries in the United States. Before the dams this stretch of the Colorado would never have harbored trout. The water temperatures then ranged from near freezing in winter to bathtub warm in the summer. The Colorado, originally named for its reddish ocher color, was so weighted down with sediment that it was said to be "too thick to drink and too thin to plough."

Now the silt settles above Glen Canyon Dam in Lake Powell. The water released to become a river comes from two hundred feet below the surface and is a constant 47°F, an ideal temperature for trout. If a person resting on a raft in the afternoon sun slips into the river, they experience a sudden temperature drop of as much as seventy degrees, a condition that can induce hypothermia within five minutes. This can be tough on clients, but it is far worse for the native fish, the chub and suckers, and the squawfish that once grew to six feet and weighed in at eighty pounds. Of the twenty-one species of fish found today in the Colorado, only six are native. Fifteen are introduced. Of the eight species once native to the canyon, five were endemic, and all of these are now moribund or extinct.

～

Water flows uphill toward money.

—Marc Reisner, *Cadillac Desert*, 1986

Motoring up the Colorado from Lees Ferry, beneath the undulating bluffs of Navajo Sandstone, exquisite and massive beyond imaginings, with the morning light on the rock and a thin veil of mist hovering over the water, one feels a strange contradiction. You want to hate this place, said by all conventional wisdom to have been ruined by the erection of the dam. And, impressive as this remnant stretch of the Glen Canyon may be, one invariably thinks of what was lost beyond the dam, the cliffs and folding sandstone of the endless chasms and canyons, the alcoves, seeps and grottos, the ruins and memories of the Anasazi, the "Ancient Ones," all drowned beneath the waters of a reservoir. And yet there is nevertheless an inherent beauty to the clear green waters, a superficial appeal in the stable stands of wispy tamarisk by the shores. It is a more welcoming river than the raging Colorado of old, with its psychotic fluctuations, its murky water impossible to bath in, let alone drink.

But this is exactly the problem. One is drawn to the modern river largely because it is so welcoming, its water clear and clean, its flows scientifically controlled and predictable. River guides here do not watch the clouds and the weather to anticipate flows. They make satellite phone calls to technicians to learn of power demands and releases, timed to the minute, with charts that measure not the frontier reaches of dreams and the imagination but the precise and certain trajectories of the artificial tides that, once released, run down the chasm of the canyon with the predictability of a well engineered machine.

Lake Powell, its blue water shimmering against the red sandstone of the desert, has a similar disconcerting allure. I once spent several days as a guest on a luxury houseboat, scuttling over the surface of the reservoir. The two-storied vessels, which rent for $2,000 a day, come equipped with climate-controlled central air conditioning, DVD players and plasma televisions on every deck and in every room, several fully equipped bars, a well-appointed kitchen, and on the top deck a hot tub and a plastic slide. As you motor out from the marina, with its acres of ramps and moorings, increasingly distant from the shore as the reservoir drops with every month of drought, you join a steady stream of recreational machines, motor craft and houseboats of all sizes, heading like a naval convoy out onto the blue surface of a body of water at one point 186 miles long with a shoreline that would stretch from Seattle to San Diego. There are Jet Skis and racing boats everywhere, roaring from gasoline pump to gasoline pump, dragging behind them boys and girls on water skis, screaming with delight.

Some twenty-seven thousand people a year raft the Grand Canyon from Lees Ferry to Diamond Creek. More than 3.5 million come to Lake Powell, infusing the local economy with some $500 million annually. The guides on the reservoir, affable and content with their paunches, cigarettes, and coolers of beer, are of a different breed from those encountered on the river. They too are good and decent people, but their fraternity has been forged by a psychic disconnect. They seem not to notice that what they call an island is in fact a drowned butte. What they describe as a lake is a manmade reservoir, so transparently artificial that it leaves as the water recedes a white stain on the red Navajo Sandstone, as conspicuous as the ring left in a bathtub as the wash water drains. They make no mention, and perhaps given their age do not even know, of the drowned beauty, the glens and hidden recesses that lie beneath their recreational playground. The death of Glen Canyon is widely perceived by the elders of the American environmental movement as one of the most egregious acts of betrayal in the history of the country, "the greatest fraud," as photographer Eliot Porter wrote,

"ever perpetrated by responsible government on an un-
suspecting people." The jewel of a canyon, a birthright for
all, was destroyed before the American people even knew
they possessed it. "No man made artifact in all of human
history," wrote Ed Abbey, "has been hated by so many for
so long as the Glen Canyon Dam."

What is most disturbing today is to realize that the
commercial operators on Lake Powell have no memory
of what once was, nor any evident interest in the history.
The fluidity of their memory, their capacity to forget, is
complete. They and their clients seek, as Porter bitterly
remarked, "artificial thrills to lessen the drag of time, side
slipping in tight S turns at thirty miles an hour." But the
truth remains, as Eliot Porter lamented. In place of a living river is a dead reservoir, a featureless sheet of water, a
moribund basin that accumulates all the flotsam from the
surrounding land, a sink for sediments and for trash, and
a burial ground for the wild.

> *Glen Canyon…is completely different. As beautiful as any
> of the canyons, it is almost absolutely serene, an interlude for a
> pastoral flute. Except for some ripples in the upper section its
> river is wide, smooth, deep, spinning in dignified whirlpools
> and moving no more than seven or eight miles an hour. Its
> walls are the monolithic Navajo sandstone, sometimes smooth
> and vertical, rounding off to domes at the rims, sometimes
> undercut by great arched caves, sometimes fantastically eroded
> by slit side canyons, alcoves, grottoes green with redbud and
> maidenhair and with springs of sweet water.*

—Wallace Stegner, *Beyond the Hundredth Meridian*, 1954

The waters impounded by this plug of artificial stone spread back through Glen Canyon, inundating the sparkling river, swallowing its luminous cliffs and tapestry walls, and extinguishing far into the long, dim, distant future everything that gave it life. As the waters creep into the side canyons, enveloping one by one their mirroring pools, drowning their bright flowers, backing up their clear, sweet springs with stale flood water, a fine opaque silt settles over all, covering rocks and trees alike with a gray slimy ooze. Darkness pervades the canyons. Death and the thickening, umbrageous gloom takes over where life and shimmering light were the glory of the river.

—Eliot Porter, *The Place No One Knew,* 1963

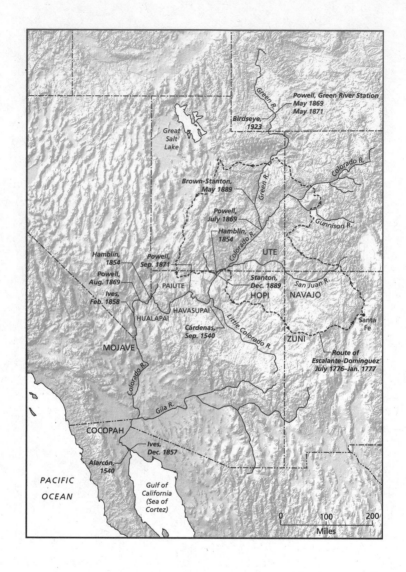

Powell, Green River Station
May 1869
May 1871

Birdseye, 1923

Green R.

Great
Salt
Lake

Colorado R.

Brown-Stanton,
May 1889

Green R.

Powell,
July 1869

Gunnison R.

Hamblin,
1854

Colorado R.

UTE

Hamblin,
1854

Powell,
Sep. 1871

Stanton,
Dec. 1889

San Juan R.

PAIUTE

HOPI

NAVAJO

Powell,
Aug. 1869

Santa
Fe

Ives,
Feb. 1858

HAVASUPAI

HUALAPAI

Little Colorado R.

ZUNI

Cárdenas,
Sep. 1540

MOJAVE

Route of
Escalante-Domínguez
July 1776–Jan. 1777

Colorado R.

Gila R.

COCOPAH

Ives,
Dec. 1857

Alarcón,
1540

PACIFIC
OCEAN

Gulf of
California
(Sea of
Cortez)

0   100   200
Miles

None but Indians have ever lived in this country, and they exist only as a part of it. They have never attempted to assert themselves, but have grown up in it like the trees. It is their food, their drink, their religion, and their life. Their songs and prayers are all of the earth, the sky and the rain. They never struggle with it, but use it to help them only as a part of themselves. They pass through it silently, leaving as little trace as sunlight through wind.

—Donald John Hall quoted in
The Place No One Knew, 1968

There is no shortage of water in the desert but exactly the right amount, a perfect ratio of water to rock, of water to sand, insuring that wide, free, open, generous spacing among plants and animals, homes and towns and cities, which makes the arid West so different from any other part of the nation. There is no lack of water here, unless you try to establish a city where no city should be.

Edward Abbey, *Desert Solitaire*, 1968

In 1539, two years before Hernando Cortes sent his cousin Francisco up the Pacific coast to look for California, a legendary kingdom of black women ruled by a queen named Caliphia, Don Francisco Vasquez de Coronado set out from Guadalajara, also heading north, with two hundred horsemen in search of Cibola, the seven cities where houses and streets were paved with gold. Like El Dorado and the Fountain of Youth, these were imaginary destinations, derived for the most part from Greek myth, and imposed by the feverish minds of the conquistadors on the virgin landscape of a new world.

Coronado's quixotic wanderings took him through lands once dominated by the Hohokam, a desert civilization that had collapsed around 1400 A.D., and across the uplands of the Mogollon Rim to the ruinous plains of West Texas, Oklahoma, and Kansas. There was no gold to be found, and no other wealth beyond the kernels of maize and the odd turquoise necklace and obsidian blade. The expedition in the end was important not for what it brought back but for what was left behind, the Arabian and Andalusian horses that allowed the peoples of the Great Plains—the Kiowa, Comanche, Arapaho, Cheyenne, Apache, Lakota, and Crow—to forge a new way of life, a hunting culture based on the buffalo and inspired by the divinity of the sun.

In the midst of his journey, a passage of deprivation and annihilation for which Coronado would be fully prosecuted under Spanish law, his second in command, Captain López de Cárdenas, stumbled upon the Grand Canyon of the Colorado, reaching the south rim somewhere between Desert View and Moran Point in late September 1540. Unimpressed and irritated by such an impediment to his progress, he stared into the abyss and saw at the bottom a narrow ribbon of water that he estimated to be a mere eight feet wide. He dispatched three of his men to investigate. They reached but a third of the way down to the canyon floor before retreating in horror and fear, their sense of scale and perspective shattered by the experience. Cárdenas later reported the canyon's existence to Coronado, dismissing it and the entire region as a "useless piece of country." The Spanish imagination was prepared and equipped to discover cities of gold, forest kingdoms of one-breasted women, and black queens. But the Grand Canyon of the Colorado was something else, a chasm that defied reason, an actual place so vast it could swallow Seville and obliterate every trace and memory.

More than two centuries would pass before another European encountered the canyon's void. In July 1776, the month America was born, two priests, Fathers Silvestre Velez de Escalante and Francisco Domínguez, set out from Santa Fe in search of an overland route through the canyon lands to Monterey, California. They never found it. Lost, beaten by the sun and frozen by winter blizzards, they survived by eating their mules and sucking the moisture from plants. The end of November found them wandering the north rim of the canyon, above Marble Canyon, seeking a crossing and a way home to the mission at Santa Fe. Cutting steps in the sandstone cliffs with an axe, they forged a route to the floor of Glen Canyon and discovered a ford, later known as the Crossing of the Fathers, which today of course lies inundated by the reservoir.

Later travelers—fur traders and trappers in the 1820s, military expeditions in the 1850s—found the region to be equally uninviting. In 1857 the War Department sent Lieutenant Joseph Christmas Ives in a stern-wheeler up the Colorado from the Gulf of California to determine the river's highest point of navigation. After two months and 350 miles he ran aground in Black Canyon, some twenty miles below the present site of Hoover Dam. Ives and his men abandoned the vessel and set off east into the Grand Canyon, exploring Diamond Creek and eventually making their way along the south rim to a point above the confluence of the main river and its notable tributary, the Little Colorado. In 1861 Ives published his expedition account, *Report Upon the Colorado River of the West*. He had not been impressed. "The region," he wrote, "is, of course, altogether valueless. It can be approached only from the south, and after entering it there is nothing to do but leave. Ours has been the first, and will doubtless be the last, party of whites to visit this profitless locality. It seems intended by nature that the Colorado River, along the greater portion of its lonely and majestic way, shall be forever unvisited and undisturbed."

The Colorado, of course, was not without worth, nor would it remain unvisited. Even as Ives ascended the river from below, there were others exploring its possibilities from above. In 1846 Brigham Young and his Mormon followers had settled the shores of the Great Salt Lake, ending an arduous pilgrimage that had taken the Latter-day

Saints across the empty wilderness of an entire continent. Their spiritual quest, like that of the many millennial religious movements that flashed in the frontier imagination of nineteenth-century America, had been born of the fantasies of a conflicted yet inspired visionary.

According to Mormon history, the founder of the faith, Joseph Smith, the son of an impoverished New England farmer, was visited in 1827 by an angel named Moroni, who presented him with golden plates inscribed with sacred messages. With the use of special stones set into silver, Smith was able to translate these metaphysical texts into the Book of Mormon. The scriptures unveiled the promise of a new religious order, a faith inspired by revelation, in which God had evolved from man, the soul predated birth, and the dead could be saved and resurrected through the rite of baptism. Among the other startling discoveries was the revealed knowledge that the tribes of Israel had migrated to the United States long before Christ. Their descendents were still alive, the myriad of Indian peoples of the American West.

Such provocative beliefs proved unsettling to some, and wherever Smith and his acolytes moved, they generated and encountered hostility. Persecution only reinforced the Mormon sense of isolation and their notion of being a chosen people, endowed with a unique mission— the building of a new world order, a new homeland. They tried Ohio and then Missouri, before settling in Illinois, where Smith oversaw the construction of the new city of Nauvoo. When, in 1844, a deranged adversary murdered Smith, his deputy, Brigham Young, decided to abandon the settled reaches of the Midwest and embark with his fellow believers on a migration west, a hegira that would not end, he vowed, until he, as the sole conduit to the angels, would receive a message from God. The destination was an imagined land of Zion, a sacred calling that in time led the Latter-day Saints not only to the shores of the Great Salt Lake but also, through a systematic plan of expansion and colonization, throughout the Great Basin and beyond.

Some colonists moved north toward Idaho and south along the Wasatch range to the far reaches of the Colorado Plateau. Other thrusts went west along the Old Spanish Trail toward Southern California, and south through Arizona to the Mexican frontier. The strategic hope of the Mormon leadership was to forge a new empire in the heart of the continent, a Kingdom of Zion, fertile, transformed, and green, with its capital to be a New Jerusalem, a shining city from where the Mormon gospel, invented in a cornfield in New England, might spread to every nation and people on earth.

At the forefront of empire were the missionary scouts, devoted frontiersmen whose duty was to explore the unknown plateaus and canyons, find sources of water in the desert, and forge alliances with the Indian nations, such that their land might be settled, and the people themselves brought into the fold of the faith. In 1854 Jacob Hamblin, a close confidant of the Mormon leader, was dispatched by Brigham Young to treat with the Paiute and find a ford of the Colorado River that might allow for the penetration of the lands of the Hopi and Navajo, and the other peoples of the southern canyons, the Havasupai and Hualapai. Hamblin found two crossings of the Colorado, one below Grand Wash Cliffs at the lower end of the Grand Canyon and another at the mouth of the Paria River, just above Marble Canyon and below the last walls of what would become known as Glen Canyon.

The Paiute were a Water People, originally from the Great Basin, who had migrated to the north rim of the canyon around 1300 A.D. A hunting and gathering culture, they lived simply in brush shelters, dependent largely on wild plants, mesquite pods, cactus fruit, and the hearts of agaves, which they rendered edible by roasting them for days in rock-lined pits under a blanket of juniper branches. Though their material culture was rudimentary, Paiute beliefs were complex and their sense of place complete. They believed that springs and rocks, rivers and rain had life spirits that had to be honored. They viewed the entire Grand Canyon as something holy. To find their way through its depths they relied on a repertoire of hundreds of songs, each a melodic road map through a sacred homeland known to them as *Puaxantu Tuvip*, words that implied a landscape vibrant and alive, responsive in a thousand ways to human needs and aspirations.

Such beliefs intrigued Jacob Hamblin, who as a missionary was sympathetic to any religious conviction, even those he intended to transform. The genesis of the Grand Canyon was to him quite obvious. The Book of Mormon made it clear that the earth, and indeed existence itself, had begun some six thousand years ago, a depth of time that was beyond the imaginings of an acolyte of a religion not yet thirty years old. The Grand Canyon, the Mormon faith maintained, had come into being in a single moment when the world had been cleaved by the earthquakes that heralded the crucifixion of Christ.

Hamblin took a Paiute woman as one of his four wives, and went on to attempt to evangelize the Hopi and the Navajo. The Navajo had come to the canyon lands late, arriving around 1600 A.D., exhausted by an epic migration that had brought them, an Athapaskan people, south in five hundred years from the northern reaches of a continent to the desert sands of the Southwest. This did not stop them from metaphysically embracing the Grand Canyon. To the contrary, even as they opportunistically learned to work silver and herd sheep, they reinvented their mythology. They already knew that their people had originated in a series of underworlds, only to emerge on the surface of a planet covered with water. When this cosmic flood receded, it left in its wake the Grand Canyon. Thus with every ritual cycle the Navajo made prayers to the canyon and the river, which was seen as an animate being, a male essence that forever flowed toward its female consort, the Little Colorado, the tributary whose waters mingled so effortlessly in the current of the greater stream.

To the Mormons such notions were nonsensical. Their mission, inspired by God, was to settle and make fertile the desert wastes. Anyone who challenged this destiny was suspect. In early September 1857 Jacob Hamblin and the apostle George A. Smith were returning from a southern sojourn, having been dispatched by Brigham

Young to warn the Mormon cadre not to engage in commerce with the wagon trains and the American settlers passing through their territory en route to the Pacific. At Corn Creek near the Utah town of Filmore, Hamblin encountered a party of families from Arkansas, led by a man named Fancher, heading west with their wagons for California. Hamblin suggested they make camp farther to the south, in the gentle grassy terrain of a place he called Mountain Meadows, not far from his own home. Then, by his account, he moved on, returning to his family in Salt Lake. Within days some 120 people in the Fancher party, every man, woman, and child old enough to speak, lay dead in the meadow, killed not by Indians but by Mormons. Only children too young to remember were spared, and these were herded for adoption into the family of the Latter-day Saints.

The perpetrators of the slaughter scattered, and the Mormon Church did little to bring them to justice. Only when word of the massacre reached Washington, and the U.S. government finally after years of passivity exerted its sovereignty, threatening the very existence of the Mormon state, did Brigham Young bring frontier justice to bear. Of all the many perpetrators, he chose to isolate one as the scapegoat, his own adopted son, John Doyle Lee, a prosperous trader and husband of nineteen women, whom he formally banished in 1870. Excommunicated from the church, Lee came south with just two of his wives to settle at the remote Colorado River crossing discovered by Jacob Hamblin just above the Paria confluence, the landing that today bears Lee's name. It was a bleak, sun-beaten flat, a devil's anvil, with no shelter from the sun. An eastern politician who later visited the site noted that he too, if dispatched to such a dreary spot, would be inclined to embrace polygamy.

Lee and his women, Rachel and Emma, arrived at the crossing in 1871 and, secretly financed by the Mormon church, immediately set to work, establishing a ferry, erecting a trading post to attract the Navajo, digging irrigation ditches, and planting fruit trees to provide a touch of shade. Emma, who was Lee's seventeenth bride, named their ranch the Lonely Dell. For a time they prospered, controlling as they did the only ferry crossing on the Colorado between Utah and California. But eventually federal law caught up with them, and John Lee was sacrificed upon the altar of Utah statehood, becoming the only Mountain Meadows murderer to be executed for his crimes. He died by firing squad on March 23, 1877. Two years later his wife Emma Lee sold the ferry for a hundred milk cows to the Mormon Church, which continued to run it until 1910, when the operation was taken over by the Coconino County government. The ferry closed in 1928, when the Navajo Bridge was built a few miles downriver across Marble Canyon. For more than fifty years Lees Ferry had provided the only access to all of the lands south of the Colorado, the conduit through which passed every Mormon missionary intent upon the transformation of all the ancient peoples of the desert—the Hopi, Navajo, Havasupai, and Hualapai and, of course, the Zuni.

~

To Zuni, the earth is alive. The walls of
Grand Canyon, the rocks, minerals and
pigments there, and the water that flows between the
walls of the canyon are all alive. Like any other
living being, the earth can be harmed, injured and
hurt when it is cut, gouged, or in other ways mistreated.
So, we believe that the Grand Canyon itself is alive and
sacred. The minerals used for pigments, the native
plants and animals mentioned in our prayers and
religious narratives, and the water of the river and its
tributaries are sacred to us and should be protected.

—Statement of the Zuni elders, 1994 annual meeting of
Western History Association, Albuquerque, New Mexico

The Zuni first saw the world when their ancestors, together with those of the Havasupai and Hualapai,
emerged from the womb of the earth near a place now
known as Ribbon Falls in the heart of the Grand Canyon. To this day their prayers recall their astonishment
as they took in the canyon's beauty, the painted rocks and
magical animals, the springs and lush plantings by the
shallows of Bright Angel Creek, the fulcrum of creation
on the canyon's rim where they first saw sunlight crack
open the sky. Inspired by what they encountered in this,
the fourth realm, the world of light, they began to wander
in search of the ideal home, *Idiwana'a*, the Middle Place,
where perfect balance and stability might be found. They

journeyed first to the east, stopping at four sacred springs, and then moved up the Little Colorado, planting corn, building villages, erecting shrines where they made offerings and buried their elders who had passed away. At the confluence of the Little Colorado and the Zuni, they encountered the *Kokko*, a host of supernatural beings. The place became sacred, encoded for all time in Zuni memory as the destination of the dead. Moving on they reached the headwaters of the river that today bears their name, the Zuni, and there they finally found *Idiwana'a*, where they settled for all time.

Countless generations later, the Zuni are still there. Their religious celebrations continue as they always have, with each ritual gesture being a prayer for the stability and prosperity of the earth and all its inhabitants. Their origin myths and all of their stories tell nothing of angels and golden tablets, or of new lands to conquer and deserts to transform. Their memories register nothing of lost tribes and chosen peoples. There is no mention of Zion in the canon of Zuni lore.

This is not to say that their mythological beliefs are any less fantastical that those of the Mormons. But it does suggest that there are different ways of interpreting reality, and that how a people conceive of themselves and their place on the earth reveals much about their values and priorities, the metaphors and intuitions that propel them forward. The Zuni accepted existence as they found it, the perfect expression of the primordial beings, Sun Father and Moonlight-Giving Mother, the ultimate custodians of light and life. They live with that knowledge and, as a consequence, have no interest in changing or improving upon the world that embraced their ancestors, and sheltered and nurtured them as infants. They look and see and accept.

The Mormons, by contrast, celebrated an ideology of transformation. The entire purpose of human life was to change the nature of the planet, rendering the wild tame, making safe and bountiful the lives of the living. Cast adrift from the lands of their origins, tormented and persecuted for a failure to conform to an orthodox world their revelations defied, they survived by becoming the absolute masters of their destiny. It was no accident that Brigham Young, inspired by the angels, elected to settle in the most barren landscape imaginable. He had asked of his flock the impossible. Through every kind of adversity and danger, they had walked the breadth of a continent, enduring tornado winds, the wrath of wild and savage tribes, the physical challenges of rivers in flood and tall-grass prairies where dense thickets of grasses rose higher than their wagons. Only a land as barren as the salt flats of Utah could provide a rough coefficient of what they had already endured and achieved, and thus redeem and affirm the fundamental truth of their spiritual convictions.

Once committed to place, they worked furiously to transform it. Their vanguard arrived at what would become Salt Lake City in the early morning of July 23, 1847. A committee of elders was appointed and by 11:30 a.m. a plot of land had been staked. By noon the first furrow had been ploughed. At two that afternoon work began on a dam and ditches that would divert water from City Creek.

By the end of the following day a five-acre field of potatoes had been planted and irrigated. Water liberated from the creek washed over the land. Their horses and cattle meanwhile grazed upon the thick wild grasses that carpeted the hillsides of the valley. Within two generations such pastures would be gone, with hardly a blade of grass to be seen. But in the valley bottomlands some six million acres would have been brought under cultivation, all by harnessing and transporting water. From the start the Mormon Church retained control of all water rights. Access to water, without which a farming family could not survive, implied fidelity and obedience to doctrine and dogma.

The success of the Mormons inspired many, most especially politicians and speculators who maintained the Jeffersonian ideal of America as a rural farming nation, in which every man might be granted his own domain, 160 acres from which to build a life. It was a proud notion, a venerable part of the American myth, and one that had worked well east of the 100th meridian. But beyond that longitude, it was sheer fantasy. As John Wesley Powell would so eloquently suggest, the issue in the west was not soil or land but water. With water, 160 acres might be too much for a man to manage. But without it even ten thousand acres, a fiefdom of a lord, could leave a family destitute. Powell's views were heretical to those calling for the settlement of the west, such as Horace Greeley, the New York newspaperman who coined the slogan, "Go West Young Man, Go West." Greeley preferred the rhetoric of men such as William Gilpin, a bombastic orator who claimed, in absolute defiance of reality, that "in readiness to receive and ability to sustain in perpetuity a dense population the west is more favored than Europe."

Promotional schemes of both government and the railroads went as far as to perpetuate the curious idea, which they cloaked in the language of nineteenth-century science, that rainfall followed the plough and that the very act of tilling the western soils would in and of itself cause rain to fall. This transparently idiotic notion was embraced through the late 1880s with the certainty of dogma. By the time such foolishness was exposed by harsh reality, it was in a sense too late. The country in defiance of all logic had become blindly committed to the agrarian settlement of the desert west. If the land itself refused to generate rain, the only option was to bring the rain to the land, and that meant irrigation on a scale previously unimagined.

In 1902, six years after Utah attained statehood, the federal government launched the United States Reclamation Service, later the Bureau of Reclamation, an agency that in time would become virtually the sole public arbiter of water policy in the states west of the 100th meridian. Inspired by the early Mormon successes, guided by Mormon laws and principles, and run in its early years largely by Mormons, the bureau set out essentially to create Zion, using all the tools of the modern state. There was, of course, interest in flood control and power generation, but the primary goal was the greening of the desert, a purpose that over time took on biblical resonance.

In 1953, President Dwight Eisenhower selected Ezra Taft Benson to become the secretary of agriculture. It was a controversial appointment. Benson's politics were rabidly conservative, far to the right of Eisenhower. He came from Utah, a state whose contribution to the farm economy at the time was trivial. Benson was also the first clergyman to be asked to serve in a presidential cabinet in more than a hundred years. Among his many published books were such titles as *Come Unto Christ; Missionaries to Match Our Message; The Constitution: A Heavenly Banner; God, Family, Country: Our Three Great Loyalties;* and *A Witness and a Warning: A Modern-Day Prophet Testifies of the Book of Mormon.* Before accepting the offer from the president of the United States, Benson had to obtain permission from the president of the Mormon Church, one David McKay. At the time of Eisenhower's offer, Benson already had a full-time job, an appointment for life as a member of the secret Quorum of the Twelve Apostles, the supreme governing body of the Church of Jesus Christ of Latter-day Saints.

Ezra Benson served Eisenhower for eight years, and played a powerful role in all policy concerning agriculture and the transformation of the desert west. He believed that the United States was a nation uniquely favored by God, and that the constitution had been divinely inspired. His zeal reflexively acknowledged that man was destined to dominate nature, possessed of a heavenly mandate to rework the earth for the benefit of all human beings, his countrymen in particular. In choosing Benson to be the face of American agriculture, Eisenhower, a son of Kansas, was sending a powerful signal that the future of farming lay in the transformation of the desert west. The key, as always in lands beyond the 100th meridian, was water. In the opening sentence to his foreword of *Water: 1955 Yearbook of Agriculture*, Benson wrote, "I have little need to remind you that water has become one of our major national concerns." With powerful figures such as Ezra Taft Benson providing inspiration and political cover, the efforts of the Bureau of Reclamation to tame the Colorado became less a technical challenge than a national mission.

In 1922 representatives of the seven states that shared the Colorado River had reached an agreement that defined and apportioned water rights and obligations. The Colorado River Compact divided the river drainage into two zones, the Upper Basin, comprising Colorado, New Mexico, Utah, and Wyoming, and the Lower Basin, which included Nevada, California, and Arizona. The goal was to divide the total water volume of the river, estimated at the time to be roughly 17.5 million acre-feet per year, equitably between the two halves of the basin. The agreement, authorized by the U.S. Congress in the same year, granted 7.5 million acre-feet annually to each of the two designated regions, leaving a reserve of 1.5 million acre-feet ultimately to satisfy the Mexicans, who also had a claim to the river. Missing from the analysis was the fact that, in time, the combined surfaces of the reservoirs on the Colorado would lose to evaporation 2 million acre-feet of water every year. What's more the figure of 17.5 million acre-feet per year was an estimate based on the observation and measurement of flows in a decade now generally recognized as having been one of abnormally high rainfall. Indeed, dendrologists suggest from the study of tree growth through time that the twentieth century may well have been the wettest in the past thousand years. The long-term flow of the Colorado is more likely to be on the order of 14.7 million acre-feet per year, a shortfall of nearly 3 million acre-feet. The recent drought, which since 1999 has resulted in reservoirs dropping to historic lows, may not be a drought at all, but merely a return to a drier climatic regime more typical of the historical pattern for the region.

None of this could have been foreseen in 1922 and, even as evidence of the miscalculation came to light in subsequent decades, no'one, certainly no state authority, rushed to return water to the commons. This was not just a matter of self-interest; it reflected an ethos unique to the West and validated by law. In the settling of America the original colonists followed the tenets of the Riparian Doctrine, old English law that stipulated that those living along a stream could use the water, provided they did not affect the flow, and thus diminish the rights of others, most especially those living downstream. In 1882 the Colorado Supreme Court repudiated this tradition in favor of the notion of prior allocation, which basically said that whoever got to the water first could claim it. Once water rights had been granted, little could be done to pry them away from the beneficiary. Thus, as these formal allotments were granted through the Colorado River Compact, they became carved in stone, and the entire thrust of state and federal government was to ensure that the obligations would be met. Further agreements, such as the

Upper Colorado River Basin Compact of 1948, empowered the Bureau of Reclamation to do whatever it deemed necessary to guarantee the delivery of water. It was, in effect, a mandate to reconfigure and envision anew the entire basin of the Colorado.

Eight years later the U.S. Congress passed the Colorado River Storage Project Act, which codified and endorsed the engineering plans proposed by the Bureau of Reclamation. The language of the bill was dense and complex, but it essentially sanctioned the construction of as many dams as were required to store in the upper reaches of the river as much water as was necessary to satisfy in perpetuity the demands and entitlements of everyone, but particularly those living in the economically thriving states of the lower river, most especially California

That such an audacious plan could even be contemplated reveals how far the engineering of massive dams had advanced in two generations. In 1900 there was not a single dam in the world higher than fifteen meters. By 1950 there were 5,270. Thirty years later there would be 36,562. Today, worldwide, there are more than eight hundred thousand dams, forty thousand of which are at least fifteen meters in height. Over the last fifty years, on average, every twelve hours has seen the construction of a dam on a scale unimaginable at the turn of the twentieth century.

The first on the Colorado, and the inspiration for all that followed, was Boulder, later known as Hoover Dam, which was initially envisioned in 1922 during the deliberations leading up to the signing of the Colorado

River Compact. The plan was to plug the Black Canyon of the Colorado with a concrete gravity arch structure of a size and height unlike anything that had ever been constructed. Authorized by Congress in 1928, the first contracts were awarded in spring 1931 to a consortium of companies, including Morrison-Knudsen of Boise, Idaho; the Utah Construction Company of Ogden, Utah; the Pacific Bridge Company of Portland, Oregon; and the Henry J. Kaiser and W.A. Bechtel companies of San Francisco and Oakland, California. None of these had ever attempted anything remotely like the task at hand. That the dam was completed in five years was a miracle of logistics and engineering, a pure act of national will.

Virtually every construction technique had to be invented on the spot by ordinary men, road builders for the most part, who knew little about dams, and what little they knew at the outset was largely irrelevant on a project of such a scale. The temporary cofferdam built to divert the river from the construction site would alone have been among the largest dams ever built had it been left standing. Excavations for the foundation of the actual dam required the removal of 1.5 million cubic yards of material. To divert the river's flow around the construction site, four tunnels, each nearly sixty feet in diameter, had to be driven a total of sixteen thousand feet through the canyon walls. The dam itself, at the time the largest structure ever built, required sixty-six million tons of concrete, as much as would be needed to build a two-lane highway from San Francisco to New York. Left alone to cure it would have taken 125 years to set because of the heat generated by the sheer weight and mass of cement. Thus it became necessary to lace the concrete with cooling coils, enough to build a refrigeration plant that would stretch from the dam site, thirty miles southeast of Las Vegas, to San Diego. When the dam was finished, the entire flow of the Colorado ran through its turbines, the water reaching speeds of some eighty-five miles per hour as it dropped through the penstocks.

An engineering marvel, Hoover Dam was stunningly beautiful, as transcendent in form and architecture as a great cathedral, with elegant Art Deco appointments and sculptured turrets rising seamlessly from its face. The monument built to celebrate the completion of the dam featured two thirty-foot winged figures of bronze, eagle images ascendant like Icarus, flanking a flagpole rising more than 140 feet from its base of black diorite stone. Surrounding the base is a terrazzo floor, inlaid with a star chart, a celestial map that recalls the alignment of the heavens on the day, September 30, 1935, when Franklin D. Roosevelt dedicated the dam. Built at the height of the Great Depression at tremendous cost of treasure and blood, Hoover Dam was more than a technical achievement. It was a symbol of national redemption and hope, a sign that in America, whatever the immediate challenges, anything could be accomplished.

Inspired as art and architecture, and producing enough electricity to bring into being entire cities in the desert, Hoover Dam was nevertheless almost immediately beset with problems, which in turn set in motion a chain reaction of further construction. Lake Mead, the reservoir created by the dam and named for Elwood Mead, who supervised its construction, spread upriver for more than a hundred miles, reaching nearly forty miles into the Grand Canyon, a broad and flat basin of water that captured every pound of Colorado River silt. Within thirty-five years Lake Mead had more acre-feet of sediment than 98 percent of the reservoirs in the United States had acre-feet of impounded water.

The solution was to build more dams, upstream. The bureau had recommended as part of the Upper Colorado Basin Project a dam at Echo Park on the Green River that would have inundated part of Dinosaur National Monument, close to the Colorado and Utah state line. The very thought of violating such a designated treasure galvanized the Sierra Club, whose members had never forgotten the damming of the Hetch Hetchy valley in Yosemite, the ecological outrage that had birthed the modern environmental movement. In a deal that he would regret for the rest of his life, David Brower, then head of the Sierra Club, agreed in 1956 not to oppose plans to dam Glen Canyon, provided the Bureau of Reclamation killed the project at Echo Park. The bureau was secretly delighted, for Glen Canyon was its priority, a site that would allow for a massive reservoir capable of storing some 24 million acre-feet, fully 80 percent of all the water of the Upper Basin. A dam at Glen Canyon would both mitigate the sediment problem in Lake Mead by capturing the silt far upstream and open up the possibility of a series of other projects reaching all through the Grand Canyon, with major dams proposed for Marble and Bridge Canyons. Had this scheme been realized, fully two-thirds of the Colorado's flow through the Grand Canyon would have stopped. The river would have become a series of reservoirs.

Work on Glen Canyon Dam began in 1959, and by September 1963, ten million tons of concrete, poured over nearly four years, had been crafted into a 710-foot-high arch and gravity dam, which curved back into the river for strength, reaching 1,560 feet across the canyon as it rose from a base 350 feet thick. The gates closed in 1963, and the waters of Lake Powell began slowly to rise, inundating the timeless beauty of Glen Canyon, the rapids of Cataract Canyon, and thousands of ancient Anasazi ruins. When the dam was formally dedicated in 1966, fourteen years before the reservoir reached its full capacity in 1980, there were no celebrations of national pride and redemption. Already the consequences of the decision to build the dam were being felt. Senator Barry Goldwater, who had secured the funds to complete the project, would later regret his decision and call the construction of the dam a mistake. Ed Abbey wrote that the flooding of Glen Canyon was the equivalent of burying the Taj Mahal or Chartres Cathedral in mud until only the spires remained visible. Abbey was not alone in later calling for the dam to be demolished.

As the public came to understand what had been sacrificed, momentum grew to protect what remained of the Grand Canyon. An advertisement placed by the Sierra Club in the *New York Times* and the *Washington Post* famously asked, "Should We Also Flood The Sistine Chapel So Tourists Can Get Nearer The Ceiling?" A sense of outrage swept through the nation, and led ultimately to the cancellation of any plans to violate the river with dams at Marble Canyon or anywhere else within the national park. As a chastened David Brower said, "If we can't save the Grand Canyon, what the hell can we save?"

Today Glen Canyon Dam remains an object of disdain. Water flows freely down the dam's corners. Hundreds of seventy-five-foot bolts have been driven into the exfoliating sandstone to pin the wall together. In 1983 it nearly collapsed. Extreme weather conditions together with a high runoff from a heavy winter snowpack brought the height of the reservoir to 3,708 feet above sea level, less than an inch below the point where engineers believed all control might have been lost. Two thousand tons of water a second roared through the spillways on either side of the dam. Ominous rumbling sounds were heard and enormous blocks of rock and concrete crashed out of the spillways. The Bureau of Reclamation issued formal statements to assure the public, but privately engineers acknowledged that they had feared for the structure's integrity. Had it collapsed, the consequences would have been catastrophic. But for some such a disaster could not have come too soon.

~

When all the rivers are used, when all the creeks in the ravines, when all the brooks, when all the springs are used, when all the reservoirs along the streams are used, when all the canyon waters are taken up, when all the artesian waters are taken up, when all the wells are sunk or dug that can be dug in all this arid region, there is still not sufficient water to irrigate all this arid region. . . . Gentlemen, it may be unpleasant for me to give you these facts. . . . I tell you, gentlemen you are piling up a heritage of conflict and litigation over water rights for there is not sufficient water to supply these lands.

—John Wesley Powell, addressing the Second International Irrigation Congress, Los Angeles, 1893

In the West when you touch water, you touch everything.

—Wayne Aspinall, congressman, Colorado Fourth District, 1949–73, Chairman House Interior and Insular Affairs Committee 1959–73

The reservoir behind Glen Canyon Dam is named for the bravest of all the river boatmen, John Wesley Powell, who led the first expedition down the Colorado River in 1869. He was a complex man who saw the promise of the West for settlement, even as he understood its limitations, given the scarcity of water and the dearth of rain. He admired what the Mormons had achieved in a generation through irrigation, but as a scientist he knew that all the water from all the rivers west of the 100th meridian would never be enough to allow the Great American Desert to bloom. He dismissed as preposterous fanciful assertions about the inherent fertility of western lands, even as he called for the rational exploitation of what water resources were to be found. As a result, a century after his great achievement on the Colorado, his legacy would be invoked both by conservationists who sought restraint and engineers who championed the complete transformation of the river that he more than anyone had elevated in the American mind. What he would have thought of the reservoir named in his honor sixty years after his death by his twentieth-century acolytes at the Bureau of Reclamation remains unclear and certainly questionable.

What is certain is that John Wesley Powell found his muse in the wild Colorado. He wrote poetically of clouds playing above the water, rolling "down in great masses, filling the gorge with gloom," or hanging "aloft from wall to wall, covering the chasm with a roof of impending storm." Another passage described a gust of wind sweeping up a draw, making a rift in the clouds to reveal all of the blue heavens, as streams of sunlight poured through, illuminating crags and pinnacles, towers and walls. "The clouds," he wrote, "are children of the heavens, and when they play among the rocks they lift them to the region above." The Grand Canyon was a wilderness of stone, he claimed, from where the gods could have quarried every mountain scattered upon the earth.

Like Walt Whitman who came a generation before him, and his contemporary John Muir, Powell was the product both of his circumstances and his own imagination, for just as the American frontier stretched the scale of the landscape, so it invited the reinvention of self. Raised the son of a poor itinerant preacher, Powell grew up literally on the open road, a wanderer. At nineteen he walked across Wisconsin, a journey of four months. A year later he rowed the length of the Mississippi, and then the Ohio and Illinois. Picking up knowledge from books and scholars encountered on the way, dropping in periodically to Wheaton and Oberlin Colleges for short sojourns, never graduating, he taught himself geology and ethnography, acquiring from direct experience the honed eye of the naturalist. Unlike more sedentary students who take what they learn in the classroom and apply it to the world, Powell absorbed unfettered what he witnessed in nature, and only later examined it through the filter of established knowledge. Thus as a scientist he saw the world as it was, not how it was expected to be, and this more than any other trait of his intellect allowed him to make unique and novel contributions to anthropology and, in particular, geology. In time he would serve as the founding director of both the U.S. Geological Survey and the Bureau of Ethnology, a singular academic achievement.

But first came the crucible of the Civil War. Powell fought for the Union, rising from private to the rank of major. At Shiloh in 1862 a minié ball shattered his right arm, which was sawn off three days after the battle, leaving him with a stump of raw nerve endings, a chronic source of acute pain for the rest of his life. Despite the agony, he served throughout the war, fighting at Big Black River at Vicksburg and all the subsequent engagements of the Mississippi campaign. When finally the war ended, in bloody exhaustion at Appomattox Court House, he like so many veterans was not about to settle down.

Accompanied by his war-crazed brother Walter, a psychic casualty of a Confederate prison camp, Powell headed for Wyoming in 1867 with the goal of exploring for the first time the one remaining blank spot on the map of the American West. The canyon lands of Utah and Arizona had been penetrated, and men had traveled up the Colorado River as far as Diamond Creek, and down from the headwaters as far as the confluence of the Green and the Grand, where at the time the Colorado proper was said to begin. But no one had attempted to go farther down into the void where the river hidden in canyons flowed for more than four hundred miles, dropping in that distance some 2,500 feet in elevation, a rate of descent twenty-five times that of the Mississippi. What Powell proposed was a journey into the unknown. Uncertainty would haunt every moment, with each bend in the river holding the promise of either deliverance or disaster.

In preparation for the expedition, Powell spent the winter of 1868–69 exploring the Green River country, living among the Ute, studying their language, all the while waiting for the spring and the arrival of his boats, which had been ordered from the east and were scheduled to be delivered on the new transcontinental railroad. The Utes clearly admired Powell, whom they named Kapurats, "the armless one." They shared with him rumors of the canyons and the river, legends of whirlpools and rapids that could swallow small mountains, caverns where the water disappeared beneath the earth to flow unimpeded through the nether reaches of the underworld. The speed and direction of the river, the character of the rapids, the possible existence of high waterfalls or cataracts capable of tearing to splinters the timber of the craft, were, in fact, as unknown to the Indians as they were to Powell.

On May 24, 1869, Powell with his party of ten men embarked at Green River Station in the Wyoming Territory. They had three 21-foot oak boats and one 16-foot pine skiff, with enough supplies to last them ten months. Before even reaching the confluence of the Grand, they lost one boat and most of their food. Within days one of the crew abandoned the expedition. Three more men would bolt from the depths of the canyon, at Separation Rapids, only to be killed three days later close to the rim, possibly by Shivwits Paiutes. Another boat, the one named for Powell's wife, the *Emma Dean*, had to be left behind on the shore. On August 30, thirteen weeks after setting out, with their supplies reduced to nothing but coffee and a few pounds of moldy flour and dried fruit, the expedition emerged from the canyon near Grand Wash. Powell and his brother Walter made their way to a Mormon settlement at the mouth of the Virgin River and left the Colorado behind. Two of his men, Andy Hall and Billy Hawkins, resupplied with food and ammunition, continued down the river to the Gulf of California, becoming the first to travel the Colorado all the way to the sea.

Powell emerged from the canyon a hero, and within days, images of him strapped into his captain's chair, his fate tied literally to that of his vessel, the *Emma Dean*, appeared in the very newspapers that only weeks before had printed premature notices of his disappearance and death. Powell amused himself on his train journey east reading his obituaries. Once back in Washington he parlayed his new fame into a congressional appropriation for a second expedition down the river. On May 22, 1871, with a decidedly more scientific team, Powell set off down the Green River, reaching Lees Ferry on October 23. They overwintered and resumed the journey on August 17, 1872, with the boatman Jack Hillers on this second leg of the exploration elevated to the position of expedition photographer. They went down the canyon as far as Kanab Creek, where on September 8, they abandoned their boats and walked out to the rim.

It would be more than two years before Powell would report his adventures in the *Scribner's Weekly*, and in that time the Grand Canyon matured in his memory, taking on a mythic quality in his imagination that completely fused his destiny with its glory. His *Report on the Exploration of the Colorado River of the West and Its Tributaries*, published by the Government Printing Office under the direction of the secretary of the Smithsonian in 1875, was written as a tale of adventure, in the first person as if a daily journal of discovery, with events from all his expeditions employed indiscriminately to build a single dramatic narrative. Powell's actual journal notes were cryptic and truncated in the extreme, as one would expect from an expedition in constant peril and chaos. In his published report deep descriptions and lyrical flourishes abound, along with engravings that inflate every feature of a landscape that by its nature already defies hyperbole. His book was conceived quite deliberately to fire the hearts of Americans, and it did, elevating Powell and the Grand Canyon, both relative unknowns at the time, to the status of American icons.

~

In the Grand Canyon, there are thousands of gorges like that below Niagara Falls, and there are a thousand Yosemites. Pluck up Mt Washington by the roots to the level of the sea and drop it headfirst into the Grand Canyon, and the dam will not force its waters over the walls. Pluck up the Blue Ridge and hurl it into the Grand Canyon, and it will not fill it.

—John Wesley Powell, *The Exploration of the Colorado River and Its Canyons,* 1987

Time, geologic time, looks out at us from the rocks as from no other objects in the landscape. Geologic time! How the striking of the great clock, whose hours are millions of years, reverberates out of the abyss of the past! Mountains fall and the foundations of the earth shift as it beats out the moments of terrestrial history. Rocks have literally come down to us from a foreworld. The youth of the earth is in the soil and in the trees and verdure that spring from it; its age is in the rocks.

—John Burroughs, *Under the Apple-Trees,* 1916

Photographs of Powell taken in his prime, with Tau-gu, his Paiute guide, in the deserts of Utah in 1872, or seated for a formal portrait as director of the Geological Survey a decade later in Washington, his long beard streaked in grey and covering his chest, suggest a leader of biblical proportions. In fact, he was a small man, 5 feet 6½ inches tall, perhaps 120 pounds fully clothed, a "stick of beef jerky adorned with whiskers," as one biographer described him. But he had immense reservoirs of ambition, confidence, and strength, and, as his shining eyes in the portraits fully attest, he suffered from a uniquely American affliction, a pathological sense of optimism that broached no possibility of failure whatever the endeavor.

Powell appreciated from the start that the story of the canyon was its geology, all of which was essentially new to science and of a scale that could well have intimidated a lesser man. But the same wild audacity that carried him downriver in the face of unimaginable perils endowed him with a quality and spirit of mind that allowed him to make sense of what he was seeing, which was no mean achievement. Even today travelers on the river, equipped with maps and books, and prompted by river guides who know the entire story by rote, still struggle to identify its features and understand its geology. Imagine how it was in Powell's day. There were no reference points; nothing on earth that could compare in scale, magnitude, and chronological depth to the world unveiled by the stratigraphy of the canyon, bands of rock that soared in places a mile above the river. At the time most of the civilized world still maintained, as did the Mormons, that the earth was six thousand years old. Scientists such as Powell were in the process of shattering that orthodoxy. In mere decades, the known age of the earth would increase a millionfold to 4.6 billion years. A million years is about fifty thousand generations. A mere hundred generations reach back to the time of Christ.

The intensity of the intellectual shock wave unleashed by these scientific discoveries can only be imagined. To accept the revelations of geology effectively obliged one to accept the revelations of biology, for if rocks could change profoundly through time, so too could species. Geology provided the time frame that the mechanics of evolutionary theory demanded. Charles Darwin published *On the Origin of Species* in 1859, a decade before Powell's Colorado expedition. The most profound and sweeping scientific theory of all time was very much on Powell's mind as he moved through the depths of the canyon. To him the entire Grand Canyon was a "library of the gods," with each of its draws and side canyons being separate reading rooms, dedicated to yet another natural wonder. "The shelves," he wrote, "are not for books, but form the stony leaves of one great book. He who would read the language of the universe may dig out letters here and there, and with them spell the words, and read, in a slow and imperfect way, but still so as to understand a little, the story of creation."

Powell did not reveal all of the mysteries of the canyon. Indeed to this day important questions remain to be answered. But given the harrowing circumstances of his passage down the river, what he discovered is astonishing.

He recognized, for example, that the river did not simply erode a path through the chasm of the canyon, but that the land itself, a vast dome of rock of the Colorado Plateau, had been soaring upward even as the river had been cutting down. Powell compared it to a saw spinning in place as the log it was cutting kept rising slowly into the blade. He recognized that a myriad of erosive forces acted on the canyon at all times. "Beds hundreds of feet in thickness and hundreds of thousands of square miles in extent," he wrote, "beds of granite and beds of schist, beds of marble and beds of sandstone, crumbling shales and adamantine lavas have slowly yielded to the silent and unseen powers of the air, and crumbled into dust and been washed away by the rains and carried into the sea by the rivers."

Perhaps most profoundly, Powell, as the writer John McPhee remarked, taught himself to think and to see in geologic time. Long before the scientific discovery of plate tectonics, before even the final acceptance of Darwinian theory, Powell envisioned the slow crawl of continents in motion, of rivers being born of rain and running into lakes that through time were as evanescent as a drop of water on a sun-baked stone. Mountains as impermanent as sand castles, oceans sweeping over the land, leaving in their wake depositions of calcium carbonate, limestone a mile thick, all composed of the remnants of organisms the size of microns. He could look up at a rock face and see a hundred million years in a glance, or take a single step down across the strata, knowing full well that his feet had traversed sixty thousand years. Time, he understood, once embraced on a scale previously unimagined, could make anything possible.

~

The finest workers in stone are not copper or steel tools, but the gentle touches of air and water working at their leisure with a liberal allowance of time.

—Henry David Thoreau, *A Week on the Concord and Merrimack Rivers*, 1873

The black gneiss below, the variegated quartzite, and the green or alcove sandstone form the foundation for the mighty red wall. The banded sandstone entablature is crowned by the tower limestone. In winter this is covered with snow. Seen from below, these changing elements seem to graduate into the heavens, and no plane of demarcation between wall and blue firmament can be seen. The heavens constitute a portion of the façade and mount into a vast dome from wall to wall, spanning the Grand Canyon with empyrean blue. So the earth and the heavens are blended in one vast structure.

—John Wesley Powell, *The Exploration of the Colorado River and Its Canyons*, 1987

Earth, we now know, was born of stardust some 4.6 billion years ago, as clouds of interstellar gas cast into the universe by the supernova explosion of a giant star spun into being the sun and all the spheres of the solar system. In the beginning there was only heat and atomic matter, the molecular foundations of existence. But within two hundred million years rocks had formed, and oceans, with a primordial crust covering the planet. Tectonic plates formed and the fundamental forces of movement, collision, subduction, and volcanic eruption gradually created the mountainous profile of the world.

Some two billion years ago a small continent that would become the nucleus of North America moved to the south and east, pushing before it an oceanic crust that slipped beneath an adjacent plate, releasing vast streams of molten magma that rose to form an arc of volcanic islands strung like fiery jewels across thousands of miles of ocean. Over the subsequent two hundred million years the continent moved closer to the islands, even as they came and went, a process of erosion and eruption that resulted in the accumulation of forty thousand feet of ash, sand, mud, and lava. When finally the continental plate drove beneath the island chain, the intense heat and pressure fused these deposits into metamorphic stone, rocks that became known to geologists as the Vishnu Schist. The magma infused in the volcanic columns and chambers solidified into Zoroaster Granite. These today form the primordial walls of the Inner Gorge of the Grand Canyon. To touch this stone is to reach back 1.8 billion years, well over a third of the history of the earth.

The tremendous mountains uplifted and forged by this collision began to erode, and by 1.2 billion years ago the Vishnu Schist and Zoroaster Granite lay fully exposed. These formations, in turn, slowly and imperceptibly slipped away, resulting after millions of years in the creation of a flat sea-level plain. An ocean then spread upon the land. Life, which had originated more than two billion years earlier, consisted still of single-celled bacteria that formed slimy mats on the sea floor. Organic and inorganic sediments from this primordial ocean created the Bass Limestone, and as the sea slipped away, the mud deposited on its retreating shores left in its wake the Hakatai Shale. These, along with the pink cliffs of Shinumo Quartzite, forged from metamorphosed river and delta sands, and the Dox Formation of sand- and mudstones, indicate that an ocean shoreline persisted in the area of the Grand Canyon until at least 1.1 billion years ago. Overlying these formations, known collectively as the Grand Canyon Supergroup, is a thick layer of Cardenas Lava, the remnants of the massive eruptions that occurred about a billion years ago as the great tectonic plates came together to form a single landmass known as Rodinia, a supercontinent that persisted for roughly 250 million years.

Then, as first Antarctica and then Australia drifted away, the sea of the west, the ancestor of the Pacific Ocean, began to expand. On land the cracking of the earth's crust created massive faults that ran as crystalline fissures across the horizons. Ground that collapsed on the downside of the faults was less exposed than that uplifted to the sun. The forces of erosion wore these latter formations down to the bone, eliminating them altogether in vast reaches of the landscape. Thus today in certain parts of the Grand Canyon, remnants of the Supergroup are readily seen and define the stratigraphy. But in other stretches along the river, where by strict chronology such formations ought to be seen, they are completely absent, and a later Paleozoic deposit, the Tapeats Sandstone, rests as a blanket directly upon the Precambrian rocks, the Vishnu Schist and Zoroaster Granite. In such places two adjacent layers of stone differ in age by as much as 1.2 billion years. This is what is known as the Great Unconformity. The rocks of the layered landscape that might speak of untold geological mysteries are simply gone, completely eroded and lost to time. If Powell's canyon is a library, and the rocks a record of a life, then half the pages of the diary have been torn asunder, leaving the reader struggling to understand the power and meaning of the slow corrosion of time.

The Paleozoic era, which began some 545 million years ago, marked a tranquil time in the history of the land that would birth the Grand Canyon. With the breakup of the Rodinia supercontinent, the region lay on a continental plate, far from tectonic activity. Erosion had left in its wake flat lowland plain, which over time was swept by the ebb and flow of the Paleozoic seas. The crystalline dust and quartz sands of the ancient beaches compressed to form the Tapeats Sandstone. Mud and clay silts carried farther from the shore settled into deeper waters, deposits that became the Bright Angel Shale. Farther out to sea, calcite, crystallized from the salt water or derived from the exoskeletons of newly evolved multicellular organisms, precipitated to form a sedimentary layer, which, once compressed by weight and time, became the Muav Limestone. These formations, collectively known as the Tonto Group, span some two hundred million years, during which time the deposits shifted as the ocean moved east, causing what had been geographically separated depositions to stack one atop the other, such that the Bright Angel Shale is seen today to lie over the Tapeats Sandstone, with the Muav Limestone forming a blanket above the shale.

Above the Tonto Group, there is another gap in time, for nowhere in the Grand Canyon is there evidence of the Ordovician or Silurian eras, a period of 130 million years that saw the birth of the flowering plants and the mass extinction of some 60 percent of marine life. In the west of the canyon Temple Butte Limestone, deposited during the late Devonian, the great age of fishes, lies above the Muav Limestone. But to the east this formation is absent and in its place is a layer deposited much later, some 350 million years ago, when oceans rose to cover virtually all of North America, and an explosion of new life brought wild diversity to the seas, the corals and bivalves, gastropods, brachiopods, crinoids, bryozoans, and all the ancient shell-bearing marine organisms that etch to this day the shadows of extinct fossil life in the imposing Redwall cliffs that dominate the canyon.

Then as the seas finally receded, leaving the limestone to crack and sink in the sun, the red sediments of the Supai Group accumulated for twenty-five million years, a time when the continent straddled the tropics and great glacial sheets reached north from the southern pole. When these in turn retreated, the land was flooded by sediments brought down from the slopes of the emergent mountains, ancestral to the Rockies. Reaching the flat plains, these rivers joined into a single somnambulant stream from which fell the muddy silts that became the Hermit Formation. These rivers of silt flowed across the region of the Grand Canyon for ten million years, but then they disappeared, and a period of intense erosion began. Huge cracks appeared in the ground, and by 270 million years ago the region had become a formidable desert as vast as the Sahara with dunes a thousand feet high. These sand dunes, which reached north as far as present-day Montana, are still seen in the sheer cliffs of Coconino Sandstone.

Inevitably the oceans returned and after five million years of desert winds the seas swept over the land. However, the air remained dry, the sun so hot that enormous volumes of salt water evaporated by the shores and above the tidal flats, leaving thick deposits of salt and gypsum that show up today in the Toroweap Formation. The sea continued to rise, and by 260 million years ago all of what is now Arizona was underwater, and once again the ocean floor was littered with the deathly remains of sponges and bivalves, corals and gastropods, a deposit that in time yielded the capstone of Powell's stratigraphic profile, the Kaibab Limestone of the canyon rim. Thus by 255 million years ago, the rocks of the modern Grand Canyon were aligned. But they were hardly in place, for they lay not as they do today at 7,000–9,000 feet, but rather at sea level, and there was as yet no river to bring their wonders to light.

The primordial continents, the great tectonic plates of Rodinia, having moved apart 750 million years ago, had after millions of years again coalesced to form the new supercontinent of Pangaea. When Pangaea in turn broke up during the Triassic, some 250 million years ago, western North America was convulsed with cataclysmic volcanic activity that brought into being entire mountain ranges. These of course inevitably eroded, and sediments thousands of feet thick accumulated in the basin of Grand Canyon, compressing the organic and inorganic materials of the Kaibab depositions into limestone.

As Pangaea continued to separate into continents, North America moved westward. Its continental plate slipped over the oceanic crust of the Pacific, forging a chain of tremendous volcanoes from Mexico to Canada even as massive forces conspired to lift up the southern Rockies and the entire Colorado Plateau. What had been the swamps of a coastal plain became a high mountainous plateau, with only the underlying coal seams to recall the exotic forests of seed ferns, cycads, and giant horsetails that had darkened the shores. Exposed to intense winds and storms of the high reaches of a continent, the Mesozoic deposits eroded away, taking with them the traces of dinosaurs, and exposing the underlying Kaibab Limestone to the sun.

Still, there was no Colorado River. Some forty-five million years ago the Colorado Plateau might have resembled contemporary Tibet, a high basin, surrounded by rings of mountains, with all streams running down to a series of enormous shallow lakes that ebbed and flowed with the seasonal snowmelt. Where the Grand Canyon is today, the rivers ran to the northeast to a lake the remnants of which are the sedimentary spires of Bryce Canyon National Park. The headwaters of the Colorado were forged relatively early, perhaps as long ago as forty-five million years. But the present course of the river was not established until a mere five million years ago. How this occurred is uncertain, but the accepted theory suggests that what became the Colorado flowed through Marble Canyon but then turned south, away from the Grand Canyon and up the drainage of what is today the Little Colorado. Near the present area of Lake Mead a stream known as the Hualapai Drainage ran from a steep escarpment all the way west to the Gulf of California. The source of that river eroded, carving its way up and into what became the Grand Canyon, until eventually it breached the last divide separating it from the upper Colorado, thus forging a single path to the sea.

There remained but a single act to the drama. Seismic eruptions beginning around nine million years ago left some eight hundred volcanoes scattered across the plateau south of the canyon. San Francisco Mountain, dominating the southern horizon and sacred to the Havasupai, soared as high as sixteen thousand feet when first forged from magma. Eruptions along the north rim of the canyon within the last 1.5 million years spilled molten rock into the canyon, plugging it with massive natural dams, which backed up the river for hundreds of miles. Eventually this too eroded away and the river continued its abrasive flow to the sea. One hundred seventy million cubic yards of sand and silt every year before the construction of the modern dams, three times the amount of dirt excavated to create the Panama Canal, and still over the course of a million years the slow erosive scouring deepened the river by a mere fifty feet. The metamorphic rocks of the Inner Gorge, the Vishnu Schist and Zoroaster Granite, stones half the age of the earth, do not yield readily even as the river itself reaches "down to the stillness of original time."

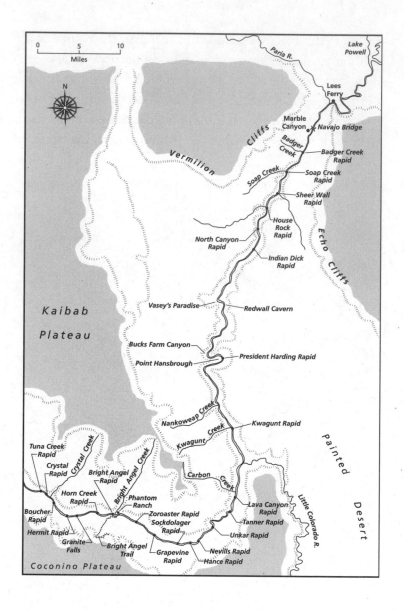

The Canyon endures the trifling busyness of humans
as it does the industry of ants, the trickle down erosion
of snow and freeze, the cascade of floods, the transient
insult of Glen Canyon Dam. These things shall pass.
The Canyon will outlive them all.

—Edward Abbey, foreword to *A River Runner's Guide to the*
History of the Grand Canyon by Kim Crumbo, 1981

The Emma *being very light is tossed about in a way*
that threatens to shake her to pieces, and is nearly as hard to
ride as a Mexican pony. We plunge along, singing, yelling,
like drunken sailors, all feeling that such rides do not come
every day. It was like sparking a black eyed girl—
just dangerous enough to be exciting.

—John C. Sumner, June 2, 1869

Within twenty miles of the river the walls of canon
gradually close in, until, in places, they reach within
fifty feet of each other. They also gain altitude, until,
at the junction of the Colorado, they tower three thousand
feet in the air. The sun is seen only three hours during the
day. Words are inadequate to describe the sensations of
one entering the tomb-like vastness.

—E.O. Beaman, *The Cañon of the Colorado*, 1874

~

As the early morning light fell upon the river at Lees Ferry, and the guides scurried about loading the rafts, I slipped away and climbed a narrow track that rose above the landing. The sound of the water soon faded, replaced by bird songs—yellow warblers, violet-green swallows, and the distant cry of a sparrow hawk. The willows and tamarisk of the riverbanks yielded to cat claw, snakeweed, opuntia, and ephedra. The shift in perspective was startling. From the heights the river ran west through a broad valley that narrowed toward infinity.

The Grand Canyon, Powell remarked, sublime though it was, demanded patience and effort to be understood. His protégé, geologist Charles Dutton, said that only the most careful of intellectual engagement would render full the wonder of the chasm. These modest reflections were never far from my mind as we finally set out down the river, for however joyous the launch and frivolous the fun of being on the water, there is for everyone who embarks on the Colorado a tremulous sense of anticipation. Too much has been said and written, too many lives transformed by the passage, for anyone to drift casually into the open embrace of the canyon.

New to the river, I felt on that first morning an odd mix of exhilaration and trepidation, not for fear of the notorious rapids, but rather out of concern that this most legendary of white-water adventures might somehow disappoint. Could a journey down a river that had by any definition been plundered and violated still inspire?

Could a place where park rangers monitor every broken twig, and where river guides and their clients, out of deference for the many thousands who would follow and camp in the same sands, comb the beaches in search of fragments of food and other micro trash, retain anything of its wild character? If not, what was one to make of this iconic canyon so revered in the American imagination? In the end, of course, the river proved me wrong, making a mockery of my myopic time frame, my parochial concerns. The splendor of the Colorado and its canyon, even today, transcends all that man has done, which is precisely why it so deserves our attention. There can surely be no greater crime against nature than to cause the death of a river, and no greater gesture of restitution than to facilitate its regeneration. In the end my passage down the Colorado and through the Grand Canyon became a cautionary tale of a river hovering in the balance, waiting to be reborn.

~

Wherever we look there is but a wilderness of rocks;
deep gorges where the rivers are lost below cliffs and
towers and pinnacles; and ten thousand strangely carved
forms in every direction; and beyond them, mountains
blending with the clouds.

—John Wesley Powell, *The Exploration of the*
Colorado River and Its Canyons, 1987

In a remarkable and unexpected way John Wesley Powell's spirit and shadow hovers over every descent. His book like a lodestone dominates the journey. The guides and crew, everyone familiar with the canyon, recite his accomplishments with reverence, pointing out landmarks, recalling from memory passages from his journals, even as those of us new to the river struggle to make sense of what he achieved. We begin at mile zero, Lees Ferry. Powell named landmarks by events and hazards of his journey, or by some poetic allusion to the inherent quality of a place, Bright Angel Creek, Separation Rapid, Marble Canyon. In 1923 a topographer with the Geological Survey, Claude Birdseye, retracing Powell's journey, brought the discipline and perspective of an engineer to the river. A bureaucratic compromise during the tangle of conflicts over water rights had arbitrarily designated Lees Ferry as the divide between the Upper and Lower Basin states. Thanks to Birdseye, numbers came to augment the lyrical language of Powell, and any feature overlooked by his original expedition was named simply for its distance in miles below Lees Ferry.

A mile below the crossing the first slabs of Kaibab Limestone mark the slow descent into the beginnings of Marble Canyon. On river right the Vermilion Cliffs shine brick red in the morning light, and to the south and west extends the Moenkopi Formation, one of the few remnants of the Mesozoic to be seen along the river. A riffle runs fast along the flank of a low bluff, churning together the clear water of the Colorado with the muddy discharge of the Paria, a stream known to the Paiutes as Elk Water. There are no rapids, though the outwash from the Paria forms a broad fan of boulders that squeezes the river toward the far shore. In 1965 two park rangers flipped their canoe in the riffle and one of them, Phillip Martin, aged twenty-seven, though wearing a life jacket, died of hypothermia. A strange fate, I thought, as we drifted past the first signs of the Toroweap sedimentary rocks, dying of cold in a desert where daytime temperatures can reach 60°F even in the heart of winter.

For all the drama of the canyon, and the intensity of its white water, there have been remarkably few fatalities on the river. Powell's expedition, of course, lost three men, but none to drowning. Until 1950 no more than a hundred people had run the river, and five years later this number had increased only to 186. In that time eleven would die. In 1962 just 372 had made the journey. By 1970 sixteen thousand people a year were heading downriver, a figure that by the end of the century would grow to well more than twenty thousand. Of the hundreds of thousands in the modern era who have come to know the Inner Gorge from waterline, only twenty have perished in rafts or kayaks. Another thirty-five have drowned swimming from shore, but these include many who died intoxicated, and several who chose suicide. Statistically, riding a commercial raft the 226 miles down to Diamond Creek, passing through 160 rapids, fifty-seven of which are serious, as the river drops 2,200 feet and the canyon walls soar overhead six thousand feet to the skyline, is one of the safest avenues of transport in the country, far less hazardous than riding a bicycle through the streets of New York City, or driving a car on the outer beltway of any American city.

But from the river it doesn't seem so safe, and this is what makes it great. On his first descent Powell smashed a hole in the side of the *Emma Dean* within hours of leaving Lees Ferry. At mile four the first traces of Coconino Sandstone appear on river left, and just beyond, below the arch of the Navajo Bridge that soars 467 feet above the river, spanning the canyon, elements of Hermit Shale grow out of the shores, again on river left. Already the canyon begins to take form, and along the banks of the river in but a few miles is displayed evidence of fifty million years of geological life. Powell saw all of this with trepidation. Recalling in his account the morning of August 5, 1869, as he passed beneath the site of what would become the Navajo Bridge, he wrote of a "feeling of anxiety we enter a new canyon this morning. We have learned to observe closely the texture of the rock. In softer strata we have a quiet river, in harder we find rapids and falls. Below us are the limestones and hard sandstones, which we found in Cataract Canyon. This bodes toil and danger."

In fact it did not, for Powell had yet to understand the nature and character of the river. In most rivers rapids form when water over time runs over a boundary between hard and soft stone, such that the latter erodes to create a drop that forms a waterfall, a chute or a cataract, a unexpected descent that can shatter a canoe. In the canyonlands, by contrast, rapids are almost invariably formed as the result of debris flows that pour out of the lateral draws and tributaries of the main channel of the river. These are not trivial events. The land is a desert, the earth parched, and yet the monsoon rains of summer can spill inches over the ground in mere minutes, as much as a foot in a day, generating flash floods that tumble and roar to the lowest point on the landscape, which almost always is a river. Thus in mere minutes tons of debris can wash down a draw at formidable speeds of as much as fifty miles per hour, creating an irresistible wall of dirt and stone that flushes into the channel and transforms the nature of the river. Though perhaps difficult to comprehend, the laws of physics suggest that the size of the stones that a flash flood can move is directly proportional to the square of the velocity of the water. If a stream's velocity quadruples due to the rush of rain, the size of rock it can carry multiplies sixteenfold. On December 4, 1966, fourteen inches of rain fell overnight and a single surge at mile ninety nine in the canyon carried hundreds of tons of debris into a modest rift in the river, washing away Anasazi ruins that had stood since the twelfth century, and transforming a minor rapid into one of the most formidable hazards on the Colorado, the rapids of Crystal Creek.

One begins to understand the meaning of water, the power of hydraulics, at the first of the serious hazards, Badger Creek Rapid, a fifteen-foot drop formed at mile eight by stones and debris flung out by Badger Creek on river right, and Jackass Creek coming in from the left. There's an oily tongue of water to follow into the rapid, immense holes, and boils and haystack waves to avoid. The place is named for an animal shot nearby by the Mormon pioneer Jacob Hamblin. He cooked it up in river water and found to his astonishment that it was so alkaline that the badger's fat turned to soap. The next day he continued south and west, passing by Ten-Mile Rock, a great vertical slab stuck like a dagger into the bed of the river, and, coming upon another cataract with a sixteen-foot drop, he named it Soap Creek. It was here that the next great stratigraphic formation of the canyon emerged, the jagged irregular walls of the Supai Sandstone. Hamblin, though he didn't know it, had stepped back in time 310 million years.

We had paused for lunch on a sandbar just below Badger, slipped down the trough of Soap Creek in the early afternoon, and come upon the death site of Frank Brown at mile twelve, a modest riffle that today bears his name. Brown was a dreamer of the American West, a railway man who set out in 1889 to build a railroad down the Grand Canyon to bring Colorado coal to California. To realize his scheme, he hired an engineer named Robert Brewster Stanton. Fortunately for all of us, the Denver, Colorado, Canyon and Pacific Railroad Company did not do well.

Ignoring Stanton's advice, Brown expedited the survey with five featherweight boats, unstable as logs, as delicate as forest leaves, easy to portage but so flimsy that two cracked in half on the train trip west. Stanton took one look at the gear assembled for the expedition and remarked very simply, "My heart sank within me." The parsimonious Brown refused to waste money on life jackets, though the technology had been proven. Stanton wanted a crew with experience. Brown treated the adventure as a lark. With all provisions for the expedition lashed on a single raft, they set out from Utah on the Green River in May 1889. Reaching Marble Canyon on July 9, they portaged Badger and made camp just downriver, above Soap Creek Rapid.

Brown awoke the following morning in a sweat. In a dream he had had a premonition of death, which that morning was realized. In a modest riffle, splattered with small harmless waves, his boat crossed an eddy line and suddenly capsized, casting Brown into a whirlpool just below Soap Creek. Weighted down with boots and heavy coat, with no life jacket, he did not have a chance. After a frantic search, the men despaired, and one of the crew, a Peter Hansbrough, inscribed an epitaph on a nearby cliff. Six days later Hansbrough and a black servant named Henry Richards set out onto the river. At the bottom of a rapid, known today as 25 Mile, the current forced them beneath an overhanging shelf. Shipping oars, they pushed off, and just when they cleared the obvious obstacles their boat flipped and both men drowned. For Stanton, a serious man, this was the tragic end of folly. He ordered the men to cache the equipment and supplies in a cave near mile thirty on the river, and then on July 17, he abandoned the canyon, leading the men on foot overland up a side canyon toward the safety of the rim. As he glanced back at the river for a final time, he saw the corpse of Frank Brown floating out of view. The following year, when Stanton, properly equipped with cork life jackets, waterproof food bags, and steady vessels, returned to the survey, setting out from Lees Ferry on Christmas

Eve 1889, he would find Hansbrough's body, planted on a rock near mile forty-three, parched and desiccated beyond recognition by the sun.

~

Leave it as it is. The ages have been at work on it, and man can only mar it. What you can do is to keep it for your children, your children's children and for all who come after you, as one of the great sights which every American, if he can travel at all, should see.

—Theodore Roosevelt, presidential address,
Grand Canyon, May 6, 1903

At mile twelve the canyon is already five hundred feet deep and the soaring bluffs reveal the distinct layers of Kaibab Limestone, the Toroweap Formation, and Coconino Sandstone, overlying a long slope of soft Hermit Shale that sweeps down to river's edge. Though the river drops only ten feet in a mile, the canyon deepens at five times that rate, for the walls on both sides incline upward at a rate of forty feet per mile. As one floats down the river, the canyon rises on all sides, and within hours of Lees Ferry one enters a hidden world that only gets deeper and more mysterious with each passing moment. At mile thirteen the river cuts through the Supai Gorge, the Esplanade Sandstone cliffs that border the river on both sides, precluding any possibility of scouting the white water. The first hazard, Sheer Wall Rapid, at the mouth of Tanner Wash, is a straightforward drop of nine feet over a shelf, but the next, House Rock, is far trickier.

The river pushes left around the wash at the mouth of Rider Canyon and along the Supai ledges of a bluff before taking a turn to the right off the rocks. All the force of the river carries the raft toward the river left and a huge standing wave, followed immediately by a tremendous hole, either of which could readily flip a boat. I row Sheer Wall, but for House Rock I am delighted to hand the oars back to my canyon guide, Shana Watahomigie, who effortlessly avoids the hazards.

Below House Rock Rapids we tie the rafts together and float for nearly two miles, until reaching Boulder Narrows, where a single massive rock divides the river. These placid stretches are typical of a river that for the most part flows at a gentle pace of five or six miles per hour. The Colorado drops 2,200 feet in the canyon, and only 10 percent of this occurs in the rapids, which are separated by, on average, a mile and a half. This still means that over the course of a two-week run there will be 160 moments of wild excitement where for short spurts the raft will plunge and buckle at speeds of up to thirty-five miles per hour, dropping as much as thirty feet in mere seconds. But most of the trip is a languid float in the sun, a time to reflect, or to chat. The guides are the very best, and they include George Wendt, a Canyon pioneer, and trip leader Regan Dale, a Californian by birth, though you would never know it. A veteran of some 250 trips down the river, Regan seems more like an Old Testament prophet. His skin is parched and freckled by the sun. His hair is cropped short as if to balance the amplitude of his thick red beard. There is always a twinkle in his eye, yet few words are spoken, and this is the key to his authority. Men parsimonious with language but active in deed inspire confidence.

Regan's family had a printing press in Riverside, California, and in 1970 it fell to him to produce an early edition of one of the first authoritative guides to the Grand Canyon. That same year, by chance, a cousin wounded in Vietnam had returned shattered by the war, and sought solace in the wild, a quest that had led him to the wilderness of the Grand Canyon. After several months, he summoned Regan from the coast, and together they discovered the river. In time Regan would become a professional guide and draft into the adventure no fewer than thirteen family members, including his wife, Ote, who runs our camps on shore, and his younger brother Tim, who without hesitation took responsibility for ferrying our mob through every hazard.

Of all the guides the person who most intrigues me is Shana, and I find myself drawn to her boat. She says little, especially in the first days, not because she is shy, as some perceive, but because she is comfortable with silence. Shana is Havasupai and one of the few Native American park rangers in Grand Canyon National Park. Known to her grandfather as Two Feathers, she grew up in a patch of pine on the south rim of the canyon, at a time when Havasupai families had to seek permission from the government to leave the 500-acre reserve that enclosed them in Cataract Creek Canyon. Her grandfather had a packing business, providing horses for tourists, and in the late 1960s he dropped off a party and then ran out of gas, only to be swept up in a bitter and unexpected November blizzard. He tried to walk into the canyon for shelter and perished. Shana's family dealt with the tragedy by clinging all the more strongly to the traditional ways.

The Havasupai, "the people of the blue green water," recognize themselves as descendants of the Anasazi, whom they call the Ancient Ones. The Havasupai know that their people have lived in the depths of the western Grand Canyon and on the uplands of the south rim for more than seven hundred years, growing crops in the canyon during the hot summer months, retreating in the fall to higher ground to forage and hunt for antelope and sheep, mule deer and wild turkeys. Other interpretations suggest that they may be descendants of the Cohonina, a culture that first appeared in the plateau country south of the canyon around 600 A.D. One legend maintains that the Pai came into existence west of the canyon at *Wikame*, or Spirit Mountain, when two fraternal deities created humans from pieces of cane. They lived together until their children fought and the parents took sides, leading the Yavapai to break away as enemies, and leaving the Havasupai and Hualapai on the rim of the canyon—two peoples, closely related in language and myth. Active trading occurred between the tribes, and with the other peoples of the canyon—the Hopi and to the west the Mojave, and in time the Navajo and Paiute. In exchange for shells and turquoise, the Havasupai offered tanned buckskin, dried agave, red ochre, and beautifully crafted baskets.

From these trading relations the Havasupai confirmed their vision of existence. The world was flat, the sky a dome that came to meet the earth around the margins of the horizons. The sky was as vast as the earth was small, and the middle of the world was the San Francisco Peaks. There were four layers to the underworld, and four to the heavens, where the sky people lived, and shamans journeyed in dreams to confront their adversaries and influence the weather. The Havasupai recognized six cardinal directions, including the zenith and the nadir, the axis of existence. In the west was found a great sea, and a land of a malevolent black spirit, who was countered by a benevolent white spirit of the east. After death the *kwidjati*, or ghosts of the dead, could return to haunt the living, and thus the Havasupai practiced cremation and never again spoke the names of those who had passed on. To ward off ghosts and disease people wore strips of porcupine skin with quills attached on hats, or a sharp piece of obsidian hanging from the neck. They listened and watched for omens—a hooting owl forewarned of a death in a family, a porcupine in the dark a harbinger of ill tidings. They healed with plants—juniper tea for diarrhea and willow sap for acne, a bit of salt for sore eyes. From Coyote they had learned the healing power of the sweat lodge, the sacred songs invented by the Wolf who took the first sweat. They believed that spirits dwelt in springs, and that the turquoise waters of Havasu Creek were as sacred as the river that formed the northern boundary of their tribal territory, the Colorado, which they considered to be the spine of the holy land of *Ha'yitad*, the homeland of their people.

The Havasupai first encountered Europeans in 1776 when a Spanish friar arrived and offered money to all those who vowed to convert to Christianity. Few did, and hostility marked all relations with the whites, culminating in open war in 1866–69. Cattle ranchers and miners encroaching from the south spurred the government to force the Havasupai from the Coconino Plateau into the narrow recesses of Havasu Creek and Cataract Canyon. In 1893 President Benjamin Harrison declared the Grand Canyon a forest preserve, a designation that Teddy Roosevelt, who famously described Native Americans as a pestilence to be removed from the plains, later elevated to the status of national monument, effectively imprisoning the Havasupai on their miniscule reservation. Missionaries, arriving in force in the late 1880s, criminalized the burning of the dead, the essential act of Havasupai funerary rites. In 1889 the people joined with the Hualapai and the Paiute and embraced the Ghost Dance, the messianic dream of a new world, replenished with game and swept clean of all white people. The vision collapsed in the face of cavalry guns.

Even as the Havasupai suffered, marginalized in their own homeland, the Grand Canyon became elevated in the American mind, the symbolic embodiment of a western landscape few in an immigrant nation were ever likely to see. It began with John Wesley Powell, whose best-selling account of the first descent of the canyon had made him a national celebrity, heralded in newspapers from coast to coast. In 1873 on his third journey west Powell brought with him the landscape artist Thomas Moran, who found in the scale and light of the canyon a means to transform nature itself into something animate, a moral force speaking for all that was good, hopeful, and pure along the wild frontiers of a new and unknown land. His majestic paintings evoked not what was, but rather what might be as progress and civilization moved inexorably to inhabit the empty expanses of the west.

More prosaically, Karl Baedeker recognized the potential of the Grand Canyon as a destination of great interest to the intrepid traveler, and he included a map of it in the 1899 edition of his guidebook to the United States. Two years later a spur of the Topeka and Santa Fe Railroad reached the canyon from the south, scuttling the stagecoach route and sparking a surge of construction that culminated in the majestic El Tovar Hotel, built with pine logs imported from Oregon. The tourist displaced the trapper, the tour guide the frontier scout. John Muir visited in 1902, the same year Buffalo Bill Cody brought a large party of British aristocrats to the north rim, with the hope that he might persuade them to buy an enormous tract as a private hunting reserve. Teddy Roosevelt came to the canyon for the first time in 1903, and he left with a tale certain to excite his many readers, a dramatic encounter with a mountain lion. "It was a wild sight," he wrote. "The maddened hounds bayed at the foot of the pine. Above them, in the lower branches, stood the horse-killing cat, the destroyer of the deer, the lord of stealthy murder, facing his doom with a heart both craven and cruel. Almost beneath him the vermillion cliffs fell silent, a thousand feet without a break. Behind him lay the Grand Canyon in its awful and desolate majesty."

Roosevelt's notion of a wilderness preserve allowed for the presence of visitors; indeed he reveled in the idea of thousands of Americans lined up along the rim of the canyon, all eager participants, as it was said, in a great democracy of awe. He famously described the canyon as "the one great sight that every American should see." But there was little place in his vision for the actual people of the land. In 1913 Roosevelt returned to the canyon five years after having declared it a national monument. He was there to hunt, keen as always to be alone in the wilderness. But as he walked down Bright Angel Trail he happened upon a number of Havasupai men and women, working their gardens by the river. The presence of natives in a protected area set aside for the American nation was quite unacceptable. According to the story, Roosevelt strolled over, formally introduced himself, and then promptly ordered the native men and women to leave. Some dismiss this account as apocryphal, but when I mentioned it to Shana, she insisted that it was true. It had happened in the lifetime of her grandparents.

Despite this history Shana feels no antagonism toward the Anglo world. She notes that the Pueblo peoples have lived in settled villages, with their languages and identities intact for seventeen hundred years. The Hopi village of Oraibi at Third Mesa has been continuously occupied for nearly nine hundred years. She reminds me that

Pueblo Bonito at Chaco Canyon, built by the Anasazi over three hundred years beginning in 800 A.D., was at its height the largest apartment complex on earth. The rituals of the Havasupai continue not for the sake of the outside world but as prayers for the survival of an enduring community. The United States, by contrast, is not yet 250 years old. When we are all gone, when the industrial spasm is exhausted, the Havasupai will still be with their children in their gardens, planting, hoeing, weeding, and harvesting the crops of their ancestors. In the meantime, Shana celebrates the Colorado, the river sacred to her people, as the lone licensed Native American guide. She has only been working the river since 2006, but her quiet confidence at the oars and her deep understanding of its moods and power suggest that the river flowed through her blood long before she first rode it toward the sea.

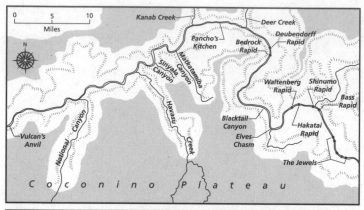

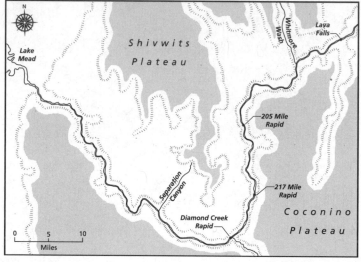

*We have cut through the sandstones and limestones
met in the upper part of the canyon, and through one
great bed of marble a thousand feet in thickness. As this
great bed forms a distinctive feature of the canyon,
we call it Marble Canyon.*

—John Wesley Powell, *The Exploration of the
Colorado River and Its Canyons*, 1987

*As the rain increased, I heard some rocks tumbling
down behind us, and, looking up, I saw one of the
grandest and most exciting scenes of the crumbling
and falling of what we so falsely call the everlasting
hills. As the water began to pour over from the plateau
above, it seemed as if the whole upper edge of the
Canyon had begun to move. Little streams, rapidly
growing into torrents, came over the hard upper stratum
from every crevice and fell on the softer slopes below. . . .
As the larger blocks of rock plunged ahead of the streams,
they crashed against other blocks, lodged on the slopes, and,
bursting with an explosion like dynamite, broke into pieces,
while the fragments flew into the air in every direction,
hundreds of feet above our heads, and as the whole
conglomerate mass of water, mud and flying rocks
came down the slopes nearer to where we were, it looked
as if nothing could prevent us from being buried in an
avalanche of rock and mud.*

—Robert Brewster Stanton, *Down the Colorado*, 1920

~

With Shana's help I try to make sense of the river. The rapids are nearly all created by debris flows coming in from lateral draws and drainages. Between the outlets of creeks and washes, where the river runs neatly past cliffs and soaring rock faces, the water is calm, a steady pulse slipping downstream at an easy pace, significantly faster than a somnambulant stream such as the Mississippi, but still a gentle, even sometimes tiresome, float. On the south rim the lay of the land leads down and away from the canyon, and thus any streams flowing into the Colorado from the left bank originate within the canyon itself, and tend to be moderate in size. The north bank tributaries, by contrast, descend from the highest heights of the canyon, with enormous forces that readily cascade boulders the size of cars and even buses into the channel of the river. Before the dams were built, the annual floods coming down the river had the power to wash away debris even of such a scale. Now the rapids build up, year by year, rock by rock, becoming ever-greater challenges. There exists the distinct possibility that one day an aggregate blockage will become so severe as to eliminate any possibility of fair passage.

Around these stones and boulders the river roars, pouring over ledges and obstacles, creating terrifying holes as the water plunges to the depths and then spins back to the surface, rushing into the very void created by the hazard and the wave. The force of the Colorado running through these rock gardens and into the deeper water spins whirlpools into being, many large enough to swallow a raft. Another dangerous dynamic occurs as the main thrust of the current runs wildly along the depths of the riverbed only to violently resurface as a boil of intense turbulence, a hydraulic surge that can threaten even a raft weighted down with a ton of gear and people. Eddy lines form below the rapids where the water by the shore reverses course and moves upstream, offering a respite from the relentless run of the river, though even these can be large enough to unsettle a raft. All of this is the natural way of water, moving down a slope. But on the Colorado the guides must watch for other signs. The volume of water brought to bear on the rocks and boulders of the rapids changes day to day, hour to hour. Every guide is aware, even in the depths of the Grand Canyon, of the well-being of Phoenix, for power demands fluctuate wildly. In 1977 there was time when the engineers deemed to release but a thousand cubic feet per second, three hundred times less than the flow of the original river at flood stage. In 1983, by contrast, they had no choice but to send ninety-three thousand cubic feet per second down the canyon. Otherwise Glen Canyon Dam might have ruptured. In riding the river, Shana tells me, your only loyalty is to the water at hand.

We camp for the first night just above North Canyon Rapid, allowing in the morning for an outing to the sunlit brilliance of a slot canyon, where the light saturates the red rock of the Supai Formation and folds of textured stone are reflected in a pool of perfectly still water. The following day we run a series of rapids known as the Roaring Twenties that carry us through the chasm of Marble Canyon, a slot that astonished Powell even as he ran in a typical day, August 9, 1869, twenty-seven rapids in thirteen miles. "The walls of the canyon, 2500 feet high," he wrote, "are of marble, of many beautiful colours, and often polished by the waves, or far up the sides where showers have washed the sands over the cliffs. At one place I have walked, for more than a mile, on a marble pavement all polished and fretted with strange devices, and embossed in a thousand fantastic patterns. Through a cleft in the wall the sun shines on this pavement, which gleams in iridescent beauty."

What Powell saw was not marble but rather his first glimpse of Redwall Limestone, the most dramatic and dominant rock feature in the Grand Canyon. Superficially, at least in color, it resembles the Navajo Sandstone of the Glen Canyon, but it is in fact a white stone, a sedimentary deposit stained red over the eons by seepage of iron oxides from the Hermit and Supai Formations that lie above it. It first appears at Indian Dick Rapid, at mile twenty-three, as a low cliff on river left. Where exposed to the river and the abrasion of sediments, it really does look like polished marble, gray not red, and sculpted into beautiful fluted forms, so exquisite that it only further saddens the spirit to recall that these formations that so beguiled Powell, and indeed everything we have seen since leaving Lees Ferry, would have been inundated had the Sierra Club not stopped plans to build the Marble Canyon Dam in the 1960s.

As we drifted into the beauty of the Redwall gorge, with the canyon closing in even as the walls soared ever higher, with dark storm clouds gathering overhead, I thought of the late David Brower, the archdruid, as he was known, who had led the fight that saved the canyon. I met him in 1971 when I was eighteen, an uncertain college freshman. He was already a legend in the environmental community, and I will always remember the day he bought me lunch, and with his wild eyes and dazzling smile, all framed by a mad shock of white hair, told me never to forget that we all had the ability to change the world. He was a great man, with a wonderful way of making people feel that they were somebody, that they could make a difference. Always remember, he cautioned, that no environmental victory is final. Nothing is ever fully protected. Every battle won only reveals new frontiers of conflict, because the forces of greed and self-interest, as he put it, always reemerge. Brower had traded Glen Canyon to secure protection for Dinosaur National Monument, only to find the Bureau of Reclamation immediately clamoring for additional dams that, if built, would have buried the entire Grand Canyon in a series of reservoirs.

As the river turns east, the Redwall becomes ever more beautiful, horizontally banded in light and dark strips, a symphony of colors, with exquisite shapes upon which shafts of light move in and out of shadow. The walls appear, as Powell wrote, as if "set with a million brilliant gems. What can it mean? Every eye is engaged, every one wonders. On coming near, we find fountains bursting from the rock, high overhead, and the spray in the sunshine forms the gems, which bedeck the wall. The rocks below the fountain are covered with mosses, and ferns and many beautiful flowering plants. We name it Vasey's Paradise in honor of the botanist who traveled with us last year."

Amid the sand of the desert, Powell had found a lush oasis of delicate plants, mosses and maidenhairs, cardinal flowers and orchids, horsetails and redbud. Out of the limestone a third of the way up the cliff face gush two jets of fresh water, which land upon stones and run away into a series of small falls. We drink from the stream and are only later reminded that the water in hand originated as rain thousands of years before, settled upon stone and slowly seeped through more than a mile of porous rock, only to gather on the impermeable layer of Muav Limestone and spout forth from the bottom of the canyon. At Vasey's Paradise, we drank the rain that had moistened fields some ten thousand years before, at the very dawn of agriculture.

The storm had gathered and great sheets of rain swept over the canyon rim. At mile thirty-three we stopped at Redwall Cavern, a vast and extraordinary chamber where the river has carved a deep and broad recess beneath the stone. In his published account Powell captivated his readers by describing it as a theatre capable of sheltering an audience of fifty thousand. A tenfold exaggeration, but the place is nevertheless astonishing, and an ideal spot to wait out a flash flood. I was sitting quietly at the far downriver end of the cavern, out of the rain but still able to see downstream where the Mauv Limestone appears along the shoreline, providing a base for the Redwall Cliffs, which form a narrow aisle, truncated by yet another face that collapses the perspective to create one of the most dramatic vistas in the canyon. Rain pounded down, and dark thunderclouds filtered the sun and an unworldly ochre glow infused the chasm. Suddenly I heard a rumbling of stone, a distant roar, that grew until, looking up, I saw fountains of water, thick with mud, explode as streams from up and down the rims of the canyon walls. A dozen dark waterfalls burst into life, sending tons of debris and slurry to the river below. These cascades grew into torrents, and the stones landed with explosive force, blasting the shores. Sloughs of debris and rocks built into small avalanches of mud and stone. Here I was witnessing the real forces that carved the canyon. Not the gentle action of sand or wind on rock, but rather massive rivers of mud, thick and powerful, capable of dislodging anything in their path, sweeping boulders as heavy as 280 tons into the river, as in fact occurred in 1990. Erosion lost all meaning as a word. This was not Thoreau's gentle march of time. This was a force capable of reconfiguring a landscape and rewriting geological history in an afternoon.

~

We camped the second night among the deer and redbud at Bucks Farm Canyon, and set out the following morning to follow the river as it turned sharply to the east to envelop the dramatic castle-like promontory of Point Hansbrough. The only moderate hazard was the President Harding Rapid, at mile forty-four, where a massive rock blocks the channel and a recent slide on river right forces the rafts to go left, around the boulder through turbulence that can flip a boat. The first sign of Bright Angel Shale appeared on river left, about three miles below the Harding Rapid, and a mile or so after that we stopped on a long beach with the hope of finding the very spot where Jack Hillers had photographed a broad historic vista, looking back up river. The goal was to ascertain through stereoscopic photography the degree to which the canyon had changed in the more than one hundred years since the Powell expedition.

In 1871 Powell had followed up the success of his initial descent of the river by pulling together a second expedition that unlike the first was manned by serious scientists and scholars. To document the journey he hired a photographer, E. O. Beaman. As both an art form and a means of documentation, photography had come into its own during the Civil War, when the battlefield images taken by Matthew Brady had so moved a nation. But the technology remained primitive, the equipment cumbersome, and the challenge of capturing images of landscape in as remote a place as the Grand Canyon was formidable. A large photograph required a large and fragile glass plate negative, which in turn implied a heavy camera mounted on a serious tripod. The colodium wet plate negatives had to be processed in the field, which demanded huge quantities of chemicals and various supplies. Beaman brought along nearly a ton of gear, including several stereoscopic cameras. In a prefilm era, these were the photographs people wanted to see, two images taken in parallel such that when viewed through an optical stereograph the landscape came alive in three dimensions. It was a technique, again coming out of the Civil War, that was used and celebrated by all the great photographers of the American West, Timothy H. O'Sullivan, William Henry Jackson, Eadweard Muybridge, and many others. Stereoscopic photography as much as any art form elevated the West in the American mind. Images of Monument Valley and Yosemite, and of course the Grand Canyon, captivated the American people, suggesting as these photographs did the existence of a land of dreams, with physical features of a scale that matched the boundless energy and ambitions of an immigrant nation soon to be the most productive and wealthy in the world.

Powell had hoped that his cousin Clem Powell would work with Beaman as an assistant, but when the young man proved to be both congenitally clumsy and lazy, he turned to a young boatman, Jack Hillers, whom he had recruited after a chance encounter in Salt Lake City. A fair-haired and blue-eyed German, an immigrant from Hanover, Hillers had fought for the Union during the war, and then at twenty-two drifted west with the regular army, rising to the rank of sergeant before taking his discharge in 1870. Powell admired the young man's strength and work ethic, his willingness to lug heavy loads of gear without complaint, and Hillers for his part took an immediate interest in the craft of photography. In 1872 Powell and Beaman had a falling out, and Powell turned to another established photographer, James Fennemore, for the second leg of the expedition. Fennemore proved too feeble for the challenges of the canyon and by midsummer, sick with fever, he was forced to abandon the party. To his credit, he had trained Hillers to take his place. Thus began a collaboration and personal friendship between Powell and Jack Hillers that would last more than thirty years, with Hillers going on to become director of photography for both the Geological Survey and the Bureau of Ethnology, and clearly one of the seminal and most celebrated American photographers of the late nineteenth century. When Powell died in 1902, Hillers was one of those chosen to carry his coffin to the grave.

Naturally it was with some anticipation that we scoured the shore and the adjacent boulder garden, searching for the exact spot where Hillers had set up his tripod and camera. The clue was a large and distinct boulder, cleft as if by design. It was uncanny to be in the very footsteps of Jack Hillers, to know that Powell no doubt had been here as well. I could not help but see the view upriver through the prism not only of this single image, but through the eyes of the photographer himself. Hillers became most famous for his portraits of Native Americans, hundreds of which are catalogued at the Bureau of Ethnology. Unlike Edward Curtis, who viewed photography as a salvage operation, posing his subjects with the explicit intention of recording the last vestiges of what he viewed as a doomed world, Hillers's portraits, especially those taken at Powell's behest among the Uinkarets and Shivwits, were of men and women in contact with the white world essentially for the first time. In the portraits their eyes look directly at Hillers, even as his lens bears down on his subjects. Standing on a stone in the canyon, discovering to our own delight that very little had changed, that the rocks and bluffs were the same, that even some trees were still alive that might have offered shade to Powell's men, I desperately wanted to know what Hillers's encounters had been like, what he had felt behind the lens, and more importantly who really were these men and women whose faces he froze in time.

~

A short day on the river, a gentle float of ten miles along Redwall and Muav Limestone with Bright Angel Shale sloping down on both banks to the river, leads to Nankoweap Delta, a broad alluvial fan built up from the debris and rock flow coming out of a canyon of the same name that issues from river right. Nankoweap is a Paiute name, first recorded by Powell, which describes a place where men fought and died, where raids occurred, and the ebb and flow of conflict bloodied the ground.

We made camp early just below the rapid, so that we would have time before dusk to scramble up the well-worn trail that rises steeply to an astonishing archaeological site, an Anasazi granary that clings like a swallow's nest to the underside of a cleft in the lower strata of the Redwall. From the heights the vista was astonishing. To the east, the fan of the delta, crisscrossed with animal trails and the faint shadowy remains of ancient gardens, bends the river into an arc that runs along the base of a canyon wall that reaches to the skyline and the rim of the canyon, located but a half mile away. To the west the rim is distant, at least seven miles as a raven flies. Looking downriver to the south, the Colorado runs away like an undulating serpent through a corridor of canyon walls. The granaries glow in the warm light, the stones and mortar set in place by human hands more than a thousand years ago have fused with the wall of the canyon and share its patina, a varnish laid down year by year, layer upon layer. There are some forty archaeological sites in Nankoweap Canyon, which date from 900 to 1100 A.D. Peering into one of the four open doors of the granary, I looked in vain for traces of Indian rice or mesquite, perhaps a kernel of maize.

Anasazi is simply a word meaning the Ancient Ones, and it refers to a culture whose history has merged with myth, such that all the living peoples associated with the canyon, the Havasupai and Zuni, the Hopi and Hualapai, feel some connection, some mystic thread of memory that links them to this common if uncertain ancestral realm. Even the Paiute and the Navajo, who demonstrably have no historical link to the Anasazi, invoke some fraternity, some lineage. For the Anasazi were not just another tribe, a mere marker indicating the ebb and flow of political and ecological fortunes in the canyon. They remain the symbol and incarnate memory of a civilization that once dominated the vast reaches of the American Southwest.

We know this much to be true from the archaeological

record. Around 400 A.D. there was an increasingly complex cultural realm in the region, a people we today rather
clumsily refer to as the Basketmakers. They practiced
agriculture, processing and grinding wild and domes-
ticated seeds with *manos* and *metates*, and hunted with
short spears and augmented the range of their weapons
with atlatls, or spear throwers. Digging sticks were used
to plant crops and to forage for roots and tubers. The dead
were buried, which implies they had notions of a spirit
realm. Within a hundred years they had learned to fire
pottery. Then, in a technological advance equivalent to
the discovery of the wheel, they developed a fast-growing,
high-yielding variety of maize, just as the climate turned
in their favor. A moist regime set in. It became possible to
produce food in surplus, which could be stored, and more
importantly controlled, thus creating the prerequisite
conditions for hierarchy and specialization, the hallmarks
of civilization.

Over the next three hundred years the Anasazi came to
live in concentrated settlements, the first villages or towns
of the American Southwest. These centers over time became interconnected as nodes in a network of roads that
linked people across an immense landscape into a single
cultural and economic sphere of life. Chaco Canyon was
the epicenter of the Anasazi world. The single complex of
Pueblo Bonito, begun in 800 A.D., was under construction for more than three hundred years. The walls stretch
for thirteen hundred feet, embracing no fewer than seven
hundred rooms clustered over five acres. The timbers of
ponderosa pine used to support the roofs of the kivas, the

circular ceremonial centers of the site, some of which are fifty-two feet in diameter and twelve feet deep, had to be transported dozens of miles across a harsh and forbidding desert landscape.

The entire complex was laid out with a master plan that aligned the lives of the living with the cosmic forces of the metaphysical realm. The movement of the heavens was captured in architecture, a geometry of sacred space that allowed windows to focus the sunlight at the summer solstice, and oriented the site throughout the year with the rising and setting of the sun. Radiating from Pueblo Bonito was a network of roads that bridged arroyos and walked up bluffs on wooden staircases or in footsteps cut into the stone. Shrines and kivas marked the routes along which fine pottery and copper bells traveled from the Zapotec, oyster shells made their way from the Gulf of Mexico, macaw feathers came up from Vera Cruz, seashells arrived from Texas and California, and turquoise and banded pipestone came south from the lands east of the Canadian Rockies, along the same route that in time would lead the Navajo down the spine of a continent into the canyon lands of the American Southwest.

At its peak the Anasazi domain included perhaps twenty thousand farmsteads, four hundred miles of monumental roads and ceremonial avenues, and no fewer than 120 urban complexes, some of which rivaled Pueblo Bonito in scale. All was well. Each year the drums and chants called forth the clouds, and the ancestral gods always answered, with rains that came every year, replenishing the fields, bringing life to the seeds. The genius and spiritual insightfulness of the priests was confirmed. At the turn of the millennium, in the year 1000 A.D., the rains were better than ever, like something from a dream, and the people rejoiced. Then in 1090 something went wrong. The prayers that had been answered for untold generations fell upon deaf ears. When the rains failed, the soil, which had been worked for more than two centuries, turned to crust. The storerooms in the great pueblos emptied. With no rain, there was no corn, and once the stored seeds had been eaten, there was nothing to replenish the fields. Drought brought in its wake starvation, and the people had no choice but to abandon their farms and begin a slow trek to wetter if less productive climes in the north.

The priests and the political elite in their desperation ordered the expansion of all construction, as if the act of building might appease the gods. Of course it failed to do so, and in the end those who survived drifted north to rekindle the elements of their lives. Some moved to the drainage of the San Juan, erecting fortified complexes such as Mesa Verde. Others found sanctuary in the canyon, where the river ran, and water could always be had. Thus in the shadow of the Redwall may be found today thousands of Anasazi sites, many as dramatic as the granaries of Nankoweap. Yet all of them echo the tragedy of Chaco Canyon, for in the desert the climate is always fickle. Within a few generations those who had settled and found respite in the canyon were chased out by an another more severe drought in the middle of the twelfth century that rendered uninhabitable even the lands on the margins of the mighty Colorado. From that point on, the canyon took on another resonance. No longer a place to live, it became a sacred destination, a point of return, where in fleeting moments all the First Nations might recall in ceremony the genius and monumental achievements of the Ancient Ones, those who had ruled the desert a thousand years before the European conquest.

~

We skirted the hole at Kwagunt Rapid, and continued down the ten miles of river that separated Nankoweap from the mouth of the Little Colorado. The tributary, the largest to enter the main stem of the river in the canyon, drains a large basin of some thirty-seven thousand square miles. Its flow is normally a radiant color, deep blue or aquamarine. Because of the rains and flash floods, it is today muddy and dark, thicker in sediments than the Colorado itself. This is how Powell found it on August 10, 1869, a foul stream, "so filthy and muddy it fairly stank." One of his crew, Jack Sumner, described the Little Colorado as being "as disgusting a stream as there is on the continent," with little but slime and mud. It was, he wrote, "a miserably lonely place indeed, with no signs of life but lizards, bats and scorpions. It seemed like the first gates of hell."

To the horror of his men, who hated the site and were anxious for home, Powell elected to hold up for several days. Much as he admired the dramatic view of Chuar Butte, which displayed in a single flank virtually the entire geological history of the canyon, he had other things on his mind. This was the point of no return. Powell knew from the Hopi that a route reached into the canyon to the upper reaches of the Little Colorado. Morale was at rock bottom. The men, as George Bradley would write in his journal, were "discontented and anxious." Powell took measure of the longitude and latitude to determine their position. His calculations revealed that they were as far south as Callville, Nevada, a modest Mormon settlement that would offer an escape from the canyon. Every mile they traveled west brought them nearer to salvation. Given the condition of the men and the meager rations that remained, every bend in the river that led in any other direction would be a potentially fatal detour. On August 13, the day they once again set out on their journey, Powell scrawled a single notation in his field notebook: "Take Obs. Capt. climbed MT." Some years later, as he prepared his journals for publication, he would remember the day more lyrically.

"We are now ready to start our way down the Great Unknown. Our boats, tied to a common stake, are chafing each other, as they are tossed by the fretful river. They ride high and buoyant, for their loads are lighter than we could desire. We have but a month's rations remaining. The flour has been resifted through the mosquito net sieve; the spoiled bacon has been dried, and the worst of it boiled; the few pounds of dried apples have been spread in the sun, and reshrunken to their normal bulk; the sugar has all melted, and gone on its way down the river; but we have a large sack of coffee. The lighting of the boats has this advantage; they will ride the waves better, and we shall have but little to carry when we make a portage.

We are three-quarters of a mile in the depths of the earth, and the great river shrinks into insignificance, as it dashes its angry waves against the walls and cliffs, that rise to the world above; but they are puny ripples, and we but pigmies, running up and down the sands, or lost among the boulders.

We have an unknown distance yet to run; an unknown river yet to explore. What falls there are, we know not; what rocks beset the channel, we know not; what walls rise over the water, we know not; Ah, well! We may conjecture many things. The men talk as cheerfully as ever; jests are bandied about freely this morning; but to me the cheer is somber and the jests are ghastly."

If the Little Colorado represented to Powell's men the very gates of hell, it was for the Hopi the point of origin of all life as well as the divine destination of the dead. Descendants of the Kayenta Anasazi, the Hopi maintained that there was a time when animals and people lived together in free and open communication, with equal roles to play as denizens of the earth. Then human vice shattered the social order and people had to move to another world. Thus the ancestors of the Hopi were condemned to travel through the darkness of the inner earth through a succession of realities until finally they emerged at Sipapu, a dome of rock by a travertine stream in the basin of what is today the Little Colorado. When the ancestors rose to the light, they saw footsteps and soon encountered *Ma'saw*, the guardian of earth and fire. *Ma'saw* allowed the people to stay, provided they vowed to act as stewards of the earth. The Hopi agreed and the covenant was sealed with a gift from *Ma'saw* of corn and a digging stick. To this day much of Hopi ritual invokes this original promise. To plant corn is to grow food, but it is also to ensure the continued well-being of the entire earth, which ultimately demands and implies the presence of water. Hopi prayers and rituals, their civic ceremonies, all ultimately pay homage to the rain, rivers, and clouds, and the sacred springs scattered throughout the canyons.

In time the Hopi clans carried the message of *Ma'saw* to every corner of the planet, before returning to the canyon lands and finally settling at what is now known as Hopi Mesa, some seventy miles to the east of the Little Colorado. In death, their spirits return to *Ma'saw* and the place of origins, traveling through the cosmic navel of Sipapu to the underworld and thence to a new existence, returning to the land of the living not as human beings but as clouds that bring rain to the parched fields. In life this ultimate journey is anticipated and honored through sacred pilgrimage. Among the deities of the rocks of the canyon is Salt Woman. Her shrine is a series of salt caves and overhangs close to the shore, just downriver from the mouth of the Little Colorado. Every Hopi male, as part of his initiation into manhood, must run the distance from Hopi Mesa, tracing the trajectory of the dead, marking the way with pictographs and prayer sticks decorated with the feathered markings of their clan. It is an arduous passage, and only those pure of heart and touched by deep humility will survive. To return alive, salt in hand, is to become a man. Today the caves are off limits to visitors, as they should be. But as the rafts drift by, the low openings in the rock sparkle with mineralization, and faint colors identify still the marks of the ancient clans upon the stone walls of a canyon that remains a spiritual anchor of Hopi life.

~

After spending most of the morning at Nankoweap, we have a short day on the river, drifting through a tight gorge of Tapeats Sandstone to a camp at Carbon Creek. It is only our fourth day on the river, and yet already the tone of the trip has shifted from the initial excitement to a more settled pace. The guides are exemplary. Each evening they hit the shore and within minutes begin a sort of silent stalk of dinner, a seemingly effortless process that leaves none of the clients even aware that these men and women, having worked the oars all day, are now furiously preparing food for a ravenous mob. No one has to be told what to do, and the easy banter among the kitchen crew belies the dozens of tasks that must be accomplished if such a gang is to be fed. The food simply appears as if summoned into being. The kayakers for their part waste not a moment on shore. Oblivious to the cold, childlike in their excitement, they push against the current, leaping and spinning, disappearing into holes, surfing the crest of formidable haystacks until spinning out into an eddy. They hang in the water until the last moments of daylight fade from the sky.

Perhaps it is the simple pattern of the days that provokes this subtle shift of mood and consciousness. On the river you have no choice but to live in the moment, hour to hour. Time drifts away altogether. Everyone slows down, sheds cares, casting off thoughts of anything but this place, this flowing river, its history, its drama. The landscape, initially as unreal and incomprehensible as a abstract painting, is gradually revealed, and people who but a few days before could not have distinguished sandstone from granite are speaking in informed awe of the purplish hue of Bright Angel Shale, the incomparable beauty of a Redwall bluff.

A mile downriver from Carbon Creek the canyon opens up dramatically as the river flows through Dox Sandstone, a soft formation laid down over a billion years ago and readily eroded over the eons. The south rim looms far ahead on the skyline, as we slip over the rapids at Lava Canyon, with the sun golden on Comanche Point, soaring over the valley on river left. The one hazardous standing wave and the big hole at Tanner Rapid are readily avoided. From there, the river opens to a broad meander that moves lazily through a basin dominated by the wings of a giant amphitheater of stepped pyramids and cliffs soaring to eight thousand feet, and named for planets and the gods, Venus and Jupiter, Rama Shrine, Apollo Temple, and Vishnu Temple.

The rapids at Unkar Creek at mile seventy-two are more formidable, a seething cauldron of whitewater where the river drops twenty-five feet and sweeps into a high cliff of dark shale on river left. Rocks at the bottom of the rapid can tear a raft to shreds, and it's imperative to stay right, hugging the inside bend. On the right-hand bank a sloping bench rises to a crown of land, where scattered stone walls indicate the site of an ancient Anasazi settlement. It seems an austere place, but in the year 1090 A.D. there would have been some forty families living here. There is a sacred kiva, and remnants of the house sites and the walls that once protected the gardens from erosion. Most likely the settlement was occupied in the winter months, when the men could fish and hunt, and sow perhaps two crops of corn, one to be harvested in the spring and a second in mid-June. The summer heat would have signaled a move to the north rim, where another crop might be planted, antelope and deer hunted, and pinyon nuts gathered through the fall. This seasonal round lasted for perhaps half a century, until in 1140 a drought, so severe and persistent that the Colorado itself may have run dry, forced the people to flee the canyon for good.

When Powell and his men left the mouth of the Little Colorado, they did so "with some eagerness and some anxiety, and some misgiving, we enter the canon below, and are carried along by the swift water through walls which rise from its very edge." Almost immediately they hit a series of rapids, three of which they felt obliged to portage, lining their boats along the shore. These most likely were Lava Canyon, Unkar and Nevills, the last a sixteen-foot drop at mile 75.5, named after Norm Nevills, who led the first commercial river trip down the canyon in 1938. Here the canyon narrows, and steep cliffs of

Shinumo Quartzite enclose a river passage that will not open up and widen to a valley for more than two hundred miles.

That night Powell camped at the head of a cataract that was, as Bradley recalled, "the worst rapid we have found today and the longest we have seen on the Colorado. The rocks are seen nearly all over it for half a mile or more—indeed the river runs through a vast pile of rocks." This was Hance, a thirty-foot drop where the water runs through a gnarly garden of massive stones spread clear across the river. Named for a solitary miner who in the 1880s dug asbestos from the grim flanks, hauling it to the rim on the backs of mules, Hance is among the most formidable rapids in the canyon.

Regan, our expedition leader, ordered our rafts to shore on river right across from the mouth of Red Canyon. On both banks beautiful cliffs of red Shinumo Quartzite rose above rust red slopes of Hakatai Shale. As we made our way up the shore past cat claw trees and mesquite to scout the rapid, Regan for the first time sounded earnest, and the very tenor of his voice leant gravity to the moment, drawing in every guide close to his side. Never before on the trip had I heard him speak in full sentences. It was a tough rapid, with huge waves, boils, and churning holes that could readily swallow a raft. He prescribed a zigzag course, which everyone committed to memory.

Hance turned out to be a great tumble of a ride, a pounding half mile of haystacks and holes that spat us almost directly into the mouth of the Upper Granite Gorge, where the entire feel and mood of the canyon is transformed. In place of rich strata of sedimentary rocks soaring to the sky, the gorge is narrow, even claustrophobic, a V-shaped cleft a thousand feet deep that runs for nearly fifty miles with neither beach nor shoreline to relieve the eye. The ancient metamorphic rocks are twisted and tormented, as if tortured by the heat and pressure that transformed them 1.6 billion years ago. The Vishnu Schist is black as coal, convoluted as if molded by some primordial artist, and running through it are seams of pink Zoroaster Granite, sparkling with quartz and mica. The walls enclose the river, channeling every sound. The roar of the rapids echoes up and down the chasm.

Powell shuddered to behold the entry to the gorge, for he was certain that metamorphic rocks implied ledges straddling the river, creating impossible falls and cataracts from which there could be no retreat. He never knew what awaited him around a bend, and the fear of coming upon a lethal drop could never have been far from his mind. It was not a trivial concern. At Grand Falls on the Little Colorado, the river plummets 185 feet, a drop higher than that of Niagara. His journal entry of August 14 records his trepidation. "The gorge is black and narrow below, red and gray and flaring above, with crags and angular projections on the walls, which, cut in many places by side canyons, seem to be a vast wilderness of rocks. Down in these grand gloomy depths we glide, ever listening, for the mad waters keep up their roar; ever watching, ever peering ahead, for the narrow canon is winding, and the river is closed in so that we can see but a few hundred yards, and what there may be below we know not."

Later that morning, as if to confirm Powell's fears, the expedition came upon the first rapid that truly horrified the men. It was, he wrote, "a perfect hell of waves." The cliffs rising directly from the shore eliminated any possibility of portaging or lining the boats, leaving no choice but to run it. "The narrow river," recalled one of his crew, "dropped smoothly and suddenly away, and then beaten to a foam plunged and boomed for a third of a mile. The boats rolled and pitched like a ship in a tornado." George Bradley added, "The waves were frightful beyond anything we have yet met and it seemed for a time that our chance to save the boats was very slim." Jack Sumner, who had fought for the Union during the war, had never in his life been more afraid. "I have been in a Calvary charge," he later wrote, "charged the batteries and stood by the guns to repel a charge. But never did my sand run so low. In fact it all ran out, but as I had to have some more grit, I borrowed it from the other boys." Powell and his men named the rapid Sockdolager, nineteenth-century slang for knockout punch. It was only the beginning of forty miles of formidable white water.

On our fifth night on the river we camped at a beach just below Sockdolager and above Grapevine. Powell chose to portage Grapevine, inching his boats up and over precipitous rocks, his men passing the night sleeping in the open, "tucked around the cliff like eve-swallows." We ran right down the middle of the slot and fell almost immediately upon a series of cataracts, 83 Mile, Zoroaster Rapid, 85 Mile, and finally Bright Angel, which left us on the shore at Phantom Ranch. There at the ranger station we rendezvoused with a couple of new crew members, and dispatched one of the lads to escort those leaving by mule train up Bright Angel Trail, a well-trodden track that leads in nine miles to the South Rim.

Powell and his exhausted crew arrived here on August 15 and had no choice but to hold over for a few days. Their boats were shattered, and they had to find wood to carve new oars. The beauty of the place, the sparkling clear creek rushing out of the mouth of an exquisite red rock canyon beneath the shade of willows and cottonwood, meant nothing to his men. The temperature soared to 116°F. They had been on the river for eighty days. They were hungry, indeed slowly starving, with only ten days of meager rations and no notion whatsoever of how far they had still to travel to escape the canyon of their despair. Morale could not have been lower. Powell fought and argued with the men all that day, first with Dunn and later with Howell. Things were falling apart. "This part of the canyon," Jack Sumner wrote, "is probably the worst hole in America, if not in the world. The gloomy black rocks drive all spirit out of a man. And the excessive drenching and hard work drive all strength out of him and leave him in a bad fix indeed. We had to move on or starve."

And so they embarked once again, as did we, heading down toward Horn Creek, a formidable run where the river drops twenty feet in a burst of massive waves. Powell reached it on August 17, 1869, in a miserable rainstorm. The men had no other clothes than what they wore. Hats were long gone. There had nothing to provide protection from either the rain or the relentless sun. "It is especially cold in the rain tonight," Powell wrote. "The little canvas we have is rotten and useless; the rubber ponchos have all been lost; we have not a blanket apiece. So we build a fire; but the rain, coming down in torrents, extinguishes it, and we sit up all night on the rocks, shivering, and are more exhausted by the night's discomfort than by the day's toil."

Unbeknownst to Powell the serious rapids were only just beginning.

~

The river is very deep, the cañon very narrow,
and still obstructed, so that there is no steady flow of
stream but the waters wheel, and roll, and boil, and
we are scarcely able to determine where we can go. Now
the boat is carried to the right, perhaps close to the wall:
again she is shot into the stream, and perhaps is dragged
over to the other side, where, caught in a whirlpool,
she spins about. We can neither land nor run as we please.
The boats are entirely unmanageable; no order in
their running can be preserved; now one, now another,
is ahead, each crew laboring for its own preservation.

—John Wesley Powell, *The Exploration of the*
Colorado River and Its Canyons, 1987

Six days into the trip, we made camp just above Granite Falls. In the evening we sought out another of Jack Hillers's locations, which I photographed just before dusk. It was a view upstream, taken from a boulder garden surrounded by white sand dunes that swept perhaps a hundred feet in elevation above the Colorado, indicating just how high the river reached before the construction of the dams eliminated the spring floods. The force of such runoff could reconfigure a beach in an instant, yet the very stones that Hillers shot remained in place, surrounded by datura in full bloom, poppies, and evening primroses, the same ephemeral plants that appear as wispy shadows in his photographs.

Regan's wife, Ote, has a botanist's love of plants, and she later guided me through the dunes, pointing out her favorite species. Like everyone in the canyon she refers to datura, a low bush with white trumpetlike flowers, always as "sacred datura," a name I find curious, as the plant is in fact the drug of choice of criminals and black magicians throughout the world. Its tropane alkaloids are powerfully psychotropic, inducing a psychotic state of delirium, marked by visions of hell fire, a sensation of flight, amnesia, and ultimately death. Shamans only occasionally and with great trepidation resort to datura when all other medicinal and spiritual interventions have failed, with the hope that in touching the realm of madness unleashed by the plant they will achieve mystical revelation. The rain priests of the Zuni employed it to communicate with the spirits of the dead, while in Europe witches used broomsticks to apply extracts of related species to the genitalia, that they might soar to the nocturnal assemblies of demons, which existed only in their minds. Calling datura "sacred" implies a sweetness and benevolence that the plant, however beautiful its radiant blossoms, most definitely does not possess. A common cause of death among those under its influence is drowning, as they attempt to slake the burning thirst invariably induced by the drug. It is not something one would want to take under any circumstances, but most especially not on the banks of a surging Colorado River.

In the morning we walked the length of Granite Falls, again on river left, scouting the best route of descent. The alluvial fan of Monument Creek spits out a boulder field that pushes the river hard against a low wall on the far bank, creating a cascade of massive waves that runs directly toward a rock island several hundred feet downriver at the bottom of the rapid. The maelstrom of white water appeared formidable. The challenge, Shana instructed me, is to enter just beyond the boulders, keeping the raft as far left as possible, to avoid the ferocious water where the waves careening off the wall collide with those moving in the opposite direction.

With Shana in the bow, I took her place at the oars and pulled slowly into the current. Clinging to her advice, I dropped the raft into the rapid and had a good run, a straight shot that flashed by in a heartbeat. It was the first significant rapid that I had rowed on the Colorado, and I was amazed by the power of the water. On many rivers, certainly most of those I had known as a guide in northern Canada, it is possible to cheat a rapid, using physical·strength and leverage on the oars to pull away from a hazard or rectify a lapse in attention or judgment. A river as powerful as the Colorado, by contrast, is completely unforgiving. The waves stand still, defiantly awaiting the rafts. Eddy lines can be ten feet across, with the water moving upstream being a foot or more lower than the river, making it virtually impossible to break across the eddy fence to return to the current. Whirlpools are not simply hydraulic sinks; they are massive black holes that seem to spin to and from the very bottom of the river. Boils rise out of nowhere, surging in places several feet above the surface. It is simply impossible to push the Colorado. You can only dance with it, placing your raft on the proper line, and hoping that you don't pop an oar or screw up your alignment to the waves as the water crashes over the bow, burying the boat, as the river carries you down.

The rapids of the Colorado, as I learned on my first full day on the oars, come at you relentlessly, as Powell to his horror discovered on August 10 when he and his crew confronted no fewer than thirty-five serious hazards in fourteen miles of river. The day before he had made four portages and run twenty-seven rapids in thirteen miles. A week later the *Emma Dean*, with Powell sitting aloft, flipped, flinging him and two of his crew into the river. Two days later, on August 21, they would face six horrendous rapids in seven miles, "a perfect hell," as Jack Sumner noted in his journal.

And so it is on this river. Just a mile below Granite, there is Hermit, a sequence of five huge standing waves, each larger than the last, such that from the crest of the fourth, the final one appears as a mountain separated by an impossible valley, a deep trough that can take as long as three seconds to descend into and rise out of, assuming, that is, that your raft makes it to the crest and does not flip. Three seconds in white water such as this can feel like eternity.

Below Hermit is Boucher, a thirteen-foot drop in the shadow of Point Sublime, which soars six thousand feet above. A mile farther down is Crystal, an easy run in Powell's day that in winter 1966 was transformed into one of the most difficult passages on the river by a massive debris flow out of the mouth of Crystal Creek on river right. The river flowing across the face of the alluvial fan pushes to the left bank, dragging any craft toward two massive and dangerous holes that flank the mouth of Slate Creek on the opposite shore. As Regan explained at the scout, it is imperative to stay to the right of these holes, a trajectory that sets you up perfectly to crash into a rock island, situated just below the rapid. Thus, in a chute that concentrates the entire Colorado and plunges the river down a twenty-five-foot drop, one must execute in the middle of the torrent a somewhat delicate move, pulling the raft away from the rock island toward river left as soon as the last hole is passed. Go left too soon and the hole will eat you. Wait a moment too long and your raft may be shredded on the island. Indecision is not an option. With Shana sitting quietly on the bow, I managed to avoid the hazards and make it through, but not before colliding with another raft, which followed perhaps a bit too closely behind us. It was not a pretty sight, but no harm was done.

Throughout a long and exciting day the rapids piled up, one after the other. First came Tuna Creek, and then the Jewels, a series of cataracts beginning at mile one hundred, Agate, Sapphire, Turquoise, Ruby, and Serpentine. I momentarily lost an oar in Sapphire, and the twelve-foot drop at Serpentine took me by surprise and nearly flung me out of the boat. The Jewels are said to be relatively easy, and they are, but a mistake in any rapid in the Grand Canyon can be dire. After running Bass and Shinumo in quick succession, I was delighted to pull into camp just below the seventeen-foot drop of the day's final rapid at mile 110. I was by then tired, wet, and cold, as was Shana. But the day had been exhilarating. I later scribbled a few notes in my journal.

"I cannot describe, nor would have ever anticipated, such a sense of release, such fun, as all sense of time fades away, all worries and concerns. I have not felt so free, so unencumbered in years. So many journeys I've made in this time, so many places have I come to know. The Sahara and the Amazon, Nepal, Benin, and Mali, Polynesia and Greenland, the Canadian Arctic and the Andes of Peru, that voyage from Fiji to New Guinea through Vanuatu and the Solomons, twice around the world, Egypt, Tanzania, India, North Africa. . . . but always my life has followed. But here it disappears. This desert, these people, this river is all that exists. Today I rowed Granite, Hermit, Boucher, Crystal, Tuna, the Jewels—Sapphire, Agate, Turquoise, Emerald, Ruby, Serpentine—and all the time these wonderful young kayakers were moving in and out of the river like dancers on the waves. Tonight the entire shore is lined with friends, all laughing and talking, sleeping in the sand under the stars."

~

Clouds are playing in the Canyon today. Sometimes
they roll down in great masses, filling the gorge with gloom;
sometimes they hang aloft from wall to wall and cover
the canyon with a roof of impending storm. . . . The clouds
are children of the heavens, and when they play among
the rocks they lift them to the region above.

—John Wesley Powell, *The Exploration of the*
Colorado River and Its Canyons, 1987

Many of the sites on the river remained to be seen, many
rapids to discover. The travertine boulders and pink granite of Elves Chasm, lush with maidenhair ferns, cardinal
flowers, and columbine. Blacktail Canyon where, stretch-
ing your arms wide, you can bridge the Great Unconformity, touching with one hand Tapeats Sandstone, laid
down some 570 million years ago, while caressing with
the other Vishnu Schist, the metamorphic rock of the Inner Gorge, forged over a billion years earlier at the very
dawn of time. The waterfalls of Deer Creek and Havasu
still awaited us, and in between we would encounter the
stunningly beautiful Muav Limestone of Matkatamiba
Canyon. The rapids would continue, with Shana running
the most difficult, Hakatai and Waltenberg, Bedrock and
Dubendorff. Along the river the ecology would gradually morph, with the plants of the Sonoran Desert—cat's
claw, mesquite, brittlebush, and barrel cactus—gradually yielding to the creosote bush, ocotillo, cholla, and

a myriad other natural denizens of the Mojave. Black-throated swifts skimmed the rapids, and in the rain one lucky morning we would be blessed with an amazing sight of peregrine falcons on the prowl, dipping and diving toward the water, swooping high only to fall instantly to the kill. Along each shore, with each passing day, as if to mock the park regulations that restricted all movement on land, we would see ever increasing numbers of desert bighorn, an animal sacred to the Havasupai, tromping down the draws, trampling vegetation, creating in a single passage game trails that one day men and women would follow.

But even as we continued downstream, camping at Pancho's Kitchen or just above the beautiful rock ledges of Sinyala Canyon, where we spent our tenth night on the river, all of our thoughts were moving ahead in anticipation of Lava Falls, the single most challenging run on the river and by reputation one of the greatest rapids in North America. In two hundred yards, we had been told, the river drops some thirty-seven feet along a gradient said to be the fastest navigable water in the Western Hemisphere. The Smithsonian once reported a speed of one hundred miles per hour, a wild exaggeration that said much about the reputation of the rapid. The National Park Service offers a more sober assessment of some twenty-five to thirty-five miles per hour, still a not insignificant rate of flow for a river.

Lava clearly intimidated and confused Powell. The night before lining his boats through the falls, an ordeal that consumed much of a day, he expressed both delight and worry in his notes. "August 24, 1869. How anxious we are to make up our reckoning every time we stop, now that our diet is confined to plenty of coffee, a very little spoiled flour and a very few dried apples! It has come to be a race for dinner. Still we make such fine progress that all hands are in good cheer, but not a moment of daylight is lost."

We camped the night before our run at National Canyon, and at dinner I mentioned to Regan that I'd like to have a go at the falls. He generously agreed, though he told me to expect a wild ride. "There are only two categories of professional river guides on the Colorado," he said with a grin, "those who have flipped in Lava and those who one day will."

In the morning as I made my way toward the kitchen for breakfast I ran into one of the veteran guides peering downstream by the water. He was checking out what he called Oracle Rock. If the rock is covered in the morning, he told me, you run the slot at Lava down the middle. If the water doesn't touch the rock at all you must go right. If half of Oracle Rock is covered and half exposed, you have a choice, and this he said was the magic. From what I could see we would be going straight down the middle.

Thirteen miles separated our campsite at National Canyon from Lava Falls, and to be honest I cannot remember much of anything from that late morning float, save a growing surge of adrenalin, part excitement, and part trepidation. I felt fear, and recognized it as a good thing. On the shore the red walls of the gorge yielded to black slopes of lava. A mile above the cataract a huge basaltic rock appeared in the river channel, a great slab that rose some fifty feet out of the water, like some ancient funerary monument. Powell had named it the Vulcan's Anvil on August 25, 1869, just as he approached the falls. On all sides he saw growing signs of the volcanic activity that had convulsed this part of the canyon, long after the river had laid down its modern course. "Great quantities of lava are seen on either side," he wrote, "and then we come to an abrupt cataract. Just over the fall a cinder cone, or extinct volcano, stands on the very brink of the canyon. What a conflict of water and fire there must have been here! Just imagine a river of molten rock, running down into a river of melted snow. What a seething and boiling of the waters; what clouds of steam rolled into the heavens!"

Powell rightly guessed that all of this molten rock, pouring into the gorge from craters scattered on the distant rim three thousand feet above, would have over time choked and blocked the canyon. A million and a half years ago there were, in fact, as many as thirteen different natural dams in this part of the canyon, the largest more than twenty-three hundred feet tall and eighty-four miles wide. Such a dam would have backed up the river well into Utah, creating a lake that would have readily drowned Lees Ferry and inundated all of Glen Canyon, more than two hundred miles upstream. Eventually, over some twenty thousand years, these natural plugs eroded away, leaving the river once again free to run to the sea. In comparison to these massive formations, the modern dams at Boulder and Glen Canyons are mere irritants, certain to be gone in a flicker of geological time. Inevitably, the river will win in the end.

~

At 32,000 cubic feet per second one thousand tons of water are moving through the river channel every second. If an average elephant weighs about five tons, this means that the flow of the river is equal to 200 elephants coming by every second. A hole in the river may take up about a third of the channel so the hydraulic dynamics of that hole are about the same as 67 elephants jumping up and down on your raft.

—Larry Stevens, quoted by Edward Dolnick,
Down the Great Unknown, 2001

The fate of the Colorado and the Grand Canyon was the last thing on my mind as Regan led us up a dirt path though a thicket of tamarisk and across a steep slide that led to a promontory high above the river from where we could scout Lava Falls. For a good five minutes he simply watched, saying nothing. No one else spoke. At the moderate flows we had been experiencing, something on the order of twelve thousand cubic feet of water tumble over Lava Falls every second. Looking down, each guide took his or her own measure of the river, finding the line, anticipating the moves that would make the difference. The curious thing about running serious whitewater is that everything goes well until it goes wrong and then it goes very wrong, very fast.

Perhaps because of my inexperience in the canyon, or

the fact that the rapid had loomed so large in my mind for so many days, or because from on high everything appears intelligible and diminished in scale, I felt oddly sanguine as I gazed down upon this legendary bit of whitewater. It was not the shelf of lava I had expected. It was simply another debris field kicked out by Prospect Canyon on the far bank of the river. I understood what I was seeing, and wasn't overly concerned until Regan began to speak. He indicated the point of entry, a tongue of water that plunged into the maelstrom, and a massive hole, impossible fully to avoid. One had to skirt it to the left, and then immediately spin the boat to come perpendicular to an enormous V-wave that would, he promised with absolute certainty, completely swamp the raft. Weighted down in an instant with at least a ton of water, you would then have to turn again to align the raft to a series of massive standing waves, any one of them capable of flipping a boat, that spat you at tremendous velocity toward a massive black boulder and a turbulent dead end of stones and white water known to the guides as the Cheese Grater. Should you end up there, Regan cautioned, all that would matter would be your survival.

I clung to his every word as I made my way back to the rafts. Shana did her best to reassure me. She told me to relax, follow my own line, and all would be well. At first the view from the water seemed utterly different, as if to mock the scout as no more than a desperate act of reassurance. But then, oddly, the two perspectives merged, and I recalled without thinking the rhythm of every river I had known. Shana, without any instructions, somehow passed to me her quiet strength and confidence. I kept seeking her advice, and she kept telling me to follow my heart.

All of this transpired in the breathless moments before we plunged into the rapid. In an instant, the full force of the cataract convulsed the raft. I pulled away from the entry hole, struggled to find the proper alignment to the V-wave, catapulted the raft over and through the remaining hazards, and finally, fully taken by the river, flew past the chaos of the Cheese Grater. In mere seconds the run was over. It had been easier than expected, largely because nothing had gone wrong. I mentioned my relief to Shana, who simply smiled. Only when I attempted to pull toward shore to ride the eddy back up to the landing where other rafts were tied did I realize that the river had left me utterly spent and exhausted. It was all I could do simply to get us to shore.

Later that night, as the entire crew assembled below the falls on a stony beach, I found my way to Regan to thank him for having given me such an opportunity. I tried to explain a few things, share with him some of my thoughts. But in the moment words failed, and all I could manage was the offer of my hand, which he accepted in a firm grasp with a smile on his face. I told him that running Lava had meant a great deal to me. He simply nodded, as if language in such a place at such a moment had no purpose.

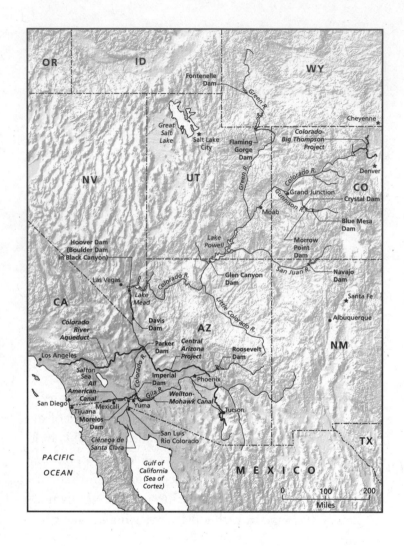

*Night and day the river flows. If time is the mind
of space, the Colorado is the soul of the desert. Brave
boatmen come, they go, they die, and the voyage
flows on forever. We are all canyoneers. We are all
passengers on this little living mossy ship, this delicate
dory sailing round the sun that humans call the earth.*

—Edward Abbey, *The Hidden Canyon: A River Journey*, 1999

*This song of waters is audible to every ear, but there is
other music in these hills, by no means audible to all . . .
On a still night, when the campfire is low and the Pleiades
have climbed over rimrocks, sit quietly and listen . . .
and think hard of everything you have seen and tried
to understand. Then you may hear it – a vast pulsing
harmony- its score inscribed on a thousand hills, its notes
the lives and deaths of plants and animals, its rhythms
spanning the seconds and the centuries.*

—Aldo Leopold, *Sand County Almanac*, 1949

*Let the mountains talk, let the river run.
Once more, and forever.*

—David Brower, *Let the Mountains Talk;
Let the Rivers Run*, 2000

~

The Grand Canyon viewed from space appears as a jagged slash on a barren landscape with a narrow filament of a river, flanked at either end by the engorged reservoirs of the Hoover and Glen Canyon Dams. On the northern side of the canyon are the dark forested heights of the Kaibab Plateau, and to the south beyond the Coconino Plateau are the San Francisco Peaks and the forested flanks of the Mogollon Rim. East of the Grand Canyon lie the kaleidoscopic sands of the Painted Desert. To the southwest the river runs away toward the clouds of the Gulf of California. In a vista encompassing thousands of square miles, the one thing that is not seen is any sign of cultivation. All the efforts of all the engineers, all the billions of dollars spent, have not turned the desert green. After a century of effort, and the construction of hundreds of dams, including twelve hundred in California alone, along with thousands of miles of aqueducts and canals, the area brought into cultivation in the entire west is roughly the size of the state of Missouri, and most of this has been made possible through the exploitation of nonrenewable ground water. The wild rivers have been sacrificed but the desert still rules the West.

Though he would go on to great fame as the director of both the Bureau of Ethnology and the U.S. Geological Survey, becoming virtually a patron saint of the Bureau of Reclamation, founded in 1902, the year of his death, John Wesley Powell, to his immense credit, recognized the limitations of desert lands. In 1893 he helped organize the Second International Irrigation Congress, which brought to Los Angeles representatives from twenty states and territories and a dozen foreign nations. Among the audience were any number of wild-eyed schemers and developers, promoters all. When Powell saw their slogan, the promise of "a million forty acre farms," all to be carved from the public domain and irrigated with the waters of the West, he became furious. Scuttling his written speech, he strode to the podium and delivered a broadside of unvarnished truth that horrified and angered many in the hall.

"I have decided on the spur of the moment," he roared, "not to present the paper I have prepared, instead I shall tell you a few facts about the arid region. I wish to make clear to you, there is not enough water to irrigate all the lands; there is not sufficient water to irrigate all the lands that could be irrigated, only a small portion can be irrigated. It is not right to speak about the area of the public domain in terms of acres that extend over the land but in terms of acres that can be supplied with water. Gentlemen it may be unpleasant for me to give you these facts. I hesitated a good deal but finally concluded to do so. I tell you gentlemen you are piling up a heritage of conflict and litigation of water rights, for there is not sufficient water to supply the land."

If only more people had heeded his message. Today the reservoirs of both Lake Mead behind Hoover Dam and Lake Powell above Glen Canyon Dam have been reduced by drought to between two-thirds and a half of their normal capacity, and scientific models suggest that they may never be full again. Snowpack in the mountains provides 90 percent of the river's flow, yet climatologists suggest that within a century 70 percent of the glaciers and snowfields may disappear entirely. The volume of water coming down the Colorado in the decade leading up to 2010 was at its lowest ebb since measurements began at Lees Ferry eighty-five years ago. Throughout the Southwest and in the basin of the Colorado, in particular, stream flows are expected to drop between 10 and 30 percent over the next decades. Long-term climate models suggest that the arid conditions of recent years may in fact be the new climatology of the region. The drought, in other words, may be here to stay.

At present more water is exported from the 250,000-square-mile basin of the Colorado River than from any other river drainage in the world. The well-being of the entire American Southwest and much of California is fully dependent on water drawn from the Colorado. The most arid states in the country are the fastest growing. The city of Phoenix alone anchors a metropolitan region of more than four million people, sprawled across a desert that receives annually less than seven inches of rain. Each year demand for water and power increases, even as the climatic regime shifts and supplies drop to new lows. In the fall of 2010 Lake Mead was 130 feet below its optimal volume. A further drop of six feet would have resulted in serious water shortages. Had reservoir levels dropped another fifty feet, the hydroelectric turbines at Hoover Dam would have been rendered inoperable. Heavy snowfall in the Rockies over the following winter offered a modest reprieve, lifting the reservoir by thirty feet to its highest level since 2009 and forestalling anticipated shortages to 2014. The city of Las Vegas is currently building a billion-dollar tunnel to the bottom of the reservoir, to be completed in 2013, so that the city and the state of Nevada will be able to continue to siphon water until the very last, even if and as Lake Mead runs dry.

Calculations and agreements hammered out in the 1920s have lost all meaning and relevance. As Brad Udall, an environmental engineer and head of the Western Water Assessment, told a Senate subcommittee in June 2007, "As we move forward all water management actions based on 'normal' as defined by the 20th century will increasingly turn out to be bad bets." Udall knows his science and his desert. His family has been around the Southwest for a very long time. His uncle, Stewart Udall, served as Secretary of the Interior under Presidents Kennedy and Johnson, and was in part responsible for the legislation that saved the Grand Canyon. His great-great-grandfather was John Doyle Lee, who founded Lees Ferry and was killed for his part in the Mountain Meadows Massacre. Brad Udall is of a new generation that will have no choice but to solve through conservation the water crisis bequeathed to it from the past. It will not be easy, but the only alternative, in the words of a prominent Western water official quoted anonymously in the *New York Times* on October 21, 2007, would be an apocalyptic collapse, in short, "an Armageddon."

~

When I last saw Shana, she shared a tragic story that nevertheless filled me with hope. Her cousin, with whom she had grown up as a sister, had suffered a terrible accident, falling to her death while observing and celebrating a lunar eclipse from the roof of a building in Reno. The family had immediately gone north to bring home the body for burial and, of equal importance to the Havasupai, to retrieve the personal effects, that they might be burned, thus eliminating any possibility that her spirit might be diverted from its sacred path and tempted to return to haunt the realm of the living. To the horror of Shana's family, the former mother-in-law, a white woman, for reasons only of spite, refused them access to the clothing and private possessions of the deceased, as well as her remains. Only after an agonizing confrontation did Shana's brother manage to persuade the estranged in-laws to release the body.

By then, it was eight days after her death, an appalling and even dangerous interval for the Havasupai. Tradition dictated that the family arrange for the funeral with utmost urgency and haste. Shana had arrived in the late afternoon and found friends and relatives gathered. The medicine man came moments later, and with sacred feathers in hand, began to sing and pray, even as Shana in her grief flung herself upon the coffin. Other ritual singers arrived, all men, and for hours they sang as the women danced. There were speeches praising the character and kindness of the deceased, and invoking by name the memory of others who had passed on, thus ensuring that Shana's cousin would not feel alone as she journeyed to the Other World. Offerings were made—blankets to warm her body, an empty bottle of Jack Daniels. A medicine woman sprinkled petals of wildflowers on the casket to cleanse the corpse and honor its spirit. What few of her possessions were at hand were then destroyed, including even the boom box that had been playing a CD of her favorite songs as the family hosted and fed the assembled guests. Nothing could remain to tempt her spirit back to the realm of the living.

The following day the family gathered on sacred ground to lay her body down. Working in shifts, the men and boys with pickaxes and digging bars chipped away a grave eight feet deep in the Kaibab Limestone of the canyon rim. A storm gathered. The rain at first evaporated before reaching the ground. But then it came down hard, pounding the earth all around the burial site. When finally, convulsed in grief, the family moved to lower the casket into the stone, a bolt of lightning struck not a hundred feet from the grave. Nothing was said, and nobody flinched, as slowly Shana's cousin was laid to rest.

On the horizon sheets of distant rain continued to fall over the canyon, but to the west there were shafts of light reaching down to the depths where the river flowed. The Havasupai will always be here, Shana told me, and the Grand Canyon will always have something to say as long as people have the hearts to listen.

What profit hath a man of all his labour, which he taketh under the sun? One generation passeth away, and another generation cometh: but the earth abideth forever. The sun also ariseth, and the sun goeth down, and hasteth to his place where he arose. The wind goeth toward the south, and turneth about unto the north; it whirleth about continually, and the wind returneth again according to his circuits. All the rivers run into the sea; yet the sea is not full; unto the place from whence the rivers come, thither they return again.

—Ecclesiastes 1:3–7

My last image of the Grand Canyon recalls the soft glowing colors of Havasu, the blue and turquoise hues of travertine stone, the green waters, and the yellow sunlight radiant in the spreading branches of a leafless tree. In the slim shadows stood Shana with her young daughter Cree, a perfect sprite of a girl, buoyant, inspired, independent, and free. One evening on the river I had asked Shana what she envisioned for her only child. In so many words she replied that Cree's future lies not in a false choice between the traditional and the modern, but rather in her right to choose the components of her life, even as she remains rooted in spirit to her ancestral lands.

Ten years before Shana was born, Havasupai elders stood united against federal proposals to plug the river between Glen Canyon and Hoover with additional dams at Marble and Bridge Canyons. The reservoir of the Bridge Canyon Dam, if built, would have flooded ninety miles of the Grand Canyon, drowning Lava Falls and all of Havasu, lands and waterfalls sacred to the Havasupai. The spiritual beliefs of the Havasupai, not to mention their fate as a people, did not register for advocates of the dams who saw in the proposed reservoirs only enhanced opportunities for recreation and tourism. As Congressman Wayne Aspinall, at the time the all-powerful chairman of the House Interior and Insular Activities Committee, remarked, "We viewed the development of the river as the only reasonable, practicable, safe, and logical way for millions of Americans and visitors to enjoy the canyon bottom which to date so few have had an opportunity to visit or view."

A native elder once told me that there are only three questions in life. Who am I? Where do I come from? And where am I going? The clash of cultures in the wake of European settlement, he suggested, was devastating for native people not only because of the terrible impact of diseases, the violence of the frontier wars, but also because the dominance and religious certainty of the newcomers allowed them to tell Indigenous peoples of every nation that their answers to these fundamental questions were wrong and had been wrong for all of their histories. Power gave credence to dogma. The central themes of the Havasupai worldview, the notion that the earth is alive, that rivers are sacred lifelines, that water itself is holy essence, were reduced to ridicule, displaced by a utilitarian ideology that maintained that such natural features only existed to be exploited for the benefit of humanity. As the Bureau of Reclamation looked forward to the building of

Hoover Dam, it dismissed the wild Colorado as but an opportunity squandered. "Unharnessed it tore through deserts, flooded fields, ravaged villages. It drained the water from the mountains and plains, and rushed it through sun-baked thirsty lands and dumped it into the Pacific Ocean—a treasure lost forever."

This government agency, established to realize the dream of Zion, the blooming of the American West, both reflected and generated the values of the frontier. In 1900, writing in *Sunset* magazine, William Smythe anticipated in similar language the promise of California's Imperial Valley. "This vast plain of opulent soil—the mighty delta of a mighty river—is rich in the potentialities of production beyond any land in our country which has ever known the plow. Yet here it has slept for ages, dormant, useless, silent. It has stood barred and padlocked against the approach of mankind. What is the key that will unlock the door to modern enterprise and human genius? It is the Rio Colorado. Whoever shall control the right to divert these turbid waters will be the master of this empire."

In 1902 the California Development Company built the Alamo Canal between Yuma, Arizona, and the Imperial Valley in California. Within two years some seventy-five thousand acres were brought into cultivation. In 1905 the Colorado, swollen by floodwaters, broke through the dikes and diversion dams. For sixteen months the entire flow of the river flooded the valley, inundating thirty thousand acres of new cropland, bringing into being the Salton Sea. The crisis prompted calls for flood control, which resulted in Hoover Dam, establishing a precedent whereby one intervention invariably led to the need for another, just as sixty years later Glen Canyon Dam would be built in part to reduce the accumulation of silt and sand that threatened the viability of Lake Mead and Hoover Dam. Each new demand on the river created a rationale for further exploitation. In 1900 the entire Los Angeles basin, land as dry as Morocco, had a population of but 130,000. San Diego was a town of less than eighteen thousand. Las Vegas did not yet exist, and only in 1930, a year before construction began on Hoover Dam, did its population surpass five thousand. Today Las Vegas and surrounding Clark County are home to nearly two million people.

That more than thirty million people now depend on the Colorado, with demands for water only growing, might suggest that attempts to change patterns of consumption, to shift priorities, for example, to allow for the restoration of the river's flow, are at best quixotic and destined to fail. Nothing in fact could be further from the truth. The fundamental dilemma in the West, as Brad Udall has written, is that we are living with nineteenth-century laws and values, twentieth-century infrastructure, and twenty-first-century water needs. But the problem is not intractable. The vast percentage of the water diverted from the Colorado does not go to water lawns in Las Vegas, fill swimming pools in San Diego, or even to grow lettuce, zucchinis, squash, peppers, cabbage, spinach, carrots, broccoli, cauliflower, bok choy, basil, and thyme beneath the desert sun at Yuma. It is overwhelmingly used for a single purpose, to fatten cattle and support a way of life rich in nostalgia but grotesquely inefficient in terms of consumption and ecological footprint.

For the last hundred years the Bureau of Land Management has been to livestock what the Bureau of Reclamation was to water. The federal agency administers 350 million acres in the West, and has set aside for cattle some 250 million acres, as much land as is found in the combined geography of all fourteen states along the Atlantic Seaboard. Yet altogether these federally permitted grazing rights support only five million head, less than ten percent of the national beef production. To maintain the cattle industry the four states of the Upper Colorado basin, Wyoming, New Mexico, Utah, and Colorado, devote fully 90 percent of the water they draw from the river to the growing of crops, and nearly 90 percent of this production is forage for cattle. In California, Arizona, and Nevada, roughly 85 percent of the water allotment goes to agriculture, with roughly half of the irrigated land again being devoted to the raising of meat. The production of a single pound of beef requires on average eighteen hundred gallons of water. The cultivation of alfalfa alone consumes 7.5 million acre-feet of water, close to half of the entire flow of the Colorado. All municipal and industrial uses combined take from the river but 630,000 acre-feet. Farmers in the Imperial Valley pay for water only $17 an acre-foot, allowing them to grow cotton, alfalfa, and rice in a desert where temperatures hover for days above 120°F and less than three inches of rain falls in a year.

Were a family in San Diego to consume water at such a rate, it would have to pay close to $1,500 for an acre-foot.

To be sure there are efficiencies to be found in every sector. In Las Vegas, where water use peaked in 2002, the city now pays residents to replace their lawns with native vegetation, and every drop of water that enters the city sewers is sanitized and returned to the reservoir at Lake Mead. In Yuma farmers are shifting to drip irrigation and questioning the wisdom of cultivating in America, for example, a grass introduced from Africa, intended only to be exported to Japan in great bales to fatten for the slaughter highly prized Kobe cattle. Of the sixteen thousand golf courses in America, one hundred fifty are in Phoenix, with each consuming a million gallons of water a day, a figure unacceptable to the most avid golfer. And surely no one can rationalize using seven hundred gallons of water and dumping into the environment half a pound of pesticides just to grow in a desert enough cotton to make a single t-shirt. Still, even assuming that all such wanton habits of consumption can be dramatically curbed, no conservation initiative can succeed that gives a free pass to the cattle industry. Indeed the entire water crisis in the American West essentially comes down to cows eating alfalfa in a landscape where neither really belongs.

～

The great symbol of the rebirth of the Colorado would be the revitalization of the river delta. Given the extent of the degradation, the time that has passed, this too may seem an impossible goal both politically and environmentally. Water would have to be found, and difficult choices made. Industrial farming and cattle interests would have to yield, and with the delta lying fully in Mexico, American authorities would have to transcend parochial concerns and act for the well-being of the river and citizens of both nations. Although this may appear a highly unlikely scenario, especially in the culturally charged landscape of the borderlands, such pessimism is actually unwarranted, for it is grounded in false assumptions about the magnitude of the challenge. The regeneration of the wetlands has, in fact, already begun, and it is unfolding at a pace and in a manner that has astonished even biologists and ecologists well versed in the resilience of nature.

As recently as the 1960s the entire Colorado delta was a barren Mexican mudflat, thanks in good measure to agricultural diversions such as the Wellton-Mohawk Irrigation and Drainage District, just across the border in Arizona, which annually siphoned off four hundred thousand acre-feet, literally sucking dry the last of the river's flow. Water that was already brackish passed through soils rich in mineral salts, resulting in groundwater so saline that it had to be pumped out from beneath the fields in the district lest it rise above the root zone and kill the crops. Roughly 120,000 acre-feet of this tainted runoff was recovered annually, mixed with river water, and assigned to Mexico's yearly allotment of 1.5 million acre-feet. Mexico naturally objected, and when its government threatened to cut off oil exports, the United States in 1974 agreed to desalinate the water before sending it south.

In Yuma the Bureau of Reclamation began construction of the world's largest reverse osmosis facility, a $250-million plant capable of treating ninety-six thousand acre-feet a year. The United States also agreed to build a $45-million drainage canal that would isolate the brackish runoff from the Wellton-Mohawk Irrigation and Drainage District and carry it fifty miles south into the Colorado delta. This was seen as a temporary measure, a gesture to placate Mexico until the desalination facility was completed. As it turned out the plant was not finished until 1992, and due to river levels and other factors, it operated only on two occasions over the subsequent decades. As a result, for more than thirty-five years a small but constant flow of water, albeit of poor quality, has flowed into one area of the delta, giving birth to a miraculous oasis known as the *Ciénega de Santa Clara*. What began in the 1970s as a small island of fertility, fed in part by natural springs, runoff, and storm surges from the sea, has grown a hundredfold to become a lush wetland covering more than forty thousand acres. Land that had been sterile for a half century took but eight years to regenerate. Today this exquisitely beautiful marsh is a refuge for thousands of migratory and resident birds, 260 species altogether, including several such as the Yuma clapper rail that hover on the brink of extinction.

Even as the *Ciénega de Santa Clara* continued to expand through the 1990s and the first decade of a new century, its survival remained precarious, completely dependent on the desalination plant at Yuma remaining idle. Should that facility have become fully operational and the diversions been curtailed, the delta would have once again been starved of water, and the renaissance marshlands most certainly would have disappeared. Fortunately by 2010, when conditions on the river did in fact oblige the desalination plant to go into continuous operation for the first time, the significance of what had begun in the delta as a serendipitous act of nature was fully appreciated by a new generation of technicians and engineers in both the United States and Mexico, and steps were taken to ensure that river water continued to reach the expanding wetlands.

As a result the regeneration of the *Ciénega de Santa Clara* has been ongoing and uninterrupted for nearly forty years, affording ecologists a remarkable opportunity to study the dynamics of a living system few ever expected to see. Their most significant discovery is how little water over time the delta actually needs to remain healthy. According to Edward Glenn, a botanist and leading authority from the University of Arizona, the natural riparian ecology would require a flow of just one-half million acre-feet every three or four years. A mere fifty thousand acre-feet would be sufficient to support gallery forests of cottonwood and willow, rich habitat for birds and wildlife. The core of the entire delta of the Colorado could be flooded with just 250,000 acre-feet of water, providing for the germination of all native vegetation. The more frequent the flows, and the greater the volume of water, the more rapid would be the expansion of the wetlands. But the bottom line is that the delta of the Colorado, the "milk and honey wilderness" of Aldo Leopold's musings, could be made whole and healthy with an annual allotment of less than one percent of the river's flow.

If nature has shown that the estuary and its verdant ecosystem *can* be reborn, science has revealed how little river water would be required for it to *be* reborn, for the heart of the Colorado delta to be returned its former glory. This presents us with a clear choice. It is one thing to lament decisions made long ago by those who are no longer with us, and whose values and priorities were forged in a very different time in the country's history. It is quite another to ignore this moment, when we have in hand the means and the knowledge to do what was once considered impossible, to bring the Colorado back from the brink, such that years from now people will remember that even as one generation compromised the river, another had the wisdom to restore it to life. What would it take to make this happen? Simply the will of the people, and the water that now goes to support a third of one percent of the nation's cattle production.

The Colorado is the American Nile, the symbol of all that the country has achieved and the promise of all that it can achieve as a wildly inventive and ever changing nation. When Wallace Stegner spoke of the geography of hope, he had in mind not just the landscape of the West, but also the spirit of a free and independent people unshackled by the past and unafraid of change. Americans of his imaginings were heroic figures who did what needed to be done and then asked whether it was possible or permissible, ordinary men and women who considered orthodoxy the enemy of invention, despair an insult to the imagination. For nearly a hundred years we have sacrificed the Colorado River on the altar of our prosperity. Surely it is time to shatter this way of thinking and recognize that the river's well-being *is* our prosperity. As Aldo Leopold wrote so long ago, when we sing of the land of the free and the brave, we must include in our lyrics the plants and the animals, the rivers and the lakes, the soil and even the stone mountains that hold up the sky. For only by doing so does the song become a hymn, and a prayer for the well-being of all, including the countless generations still waiting to be born. In their name, we must let the river flow.

Acknowledgments

My time on the Colorado was made possible by an inspired filmmaker and dedicated conservationist, Greg MacGillivray, who in 2006 invited me and my daughter Tara to be part of *Grand Canyon Adventure*, a 3D IMAX production shot on location in the canyon and throughout the Southwest. With us on the adventure were Greg's wife, Barbara; his son Shaun; my old friend Robert Kennedy Jr. and his daughter Kick; Shana Watahomigie and her daughter Cree; and an amazing crew that morphed over the weeks into an extended family, drawn together by the river. My thanks in particular go to Liz Ferrin and Angel Martinez, who made it all happen, as well as Jack Cruikshank, Regan and Ote Dale, Tim Dale, Adam Druckman, Steve Fisher, John Grace, Ben Horton, Nikki Kelly, Mark Krenzien, Doug Lavender, Katie MacGillivray, Brad Ohlund, Diana Pennington, Jack Tankard, Rob Walker, George Wendt, and Anthony Yap. In 2008, Earth Aware Editions published *Grand Canyon: River at Risk*, a limited-edition photo book conceived to support the release of the film. My thanks on that project go to Chris Rainier, and to Peter Beren, MacDuff Everton, Jake Gerli, Raoul Goff, Michael Nichols, Chris Palmer, and Lori Rick. At Island Press, I would like to thank my editor, David Miller, Chuck Savitt, Jaime Jennings, Sharis Simonian, Rebecca Bright, and Avery Murphy. At Greystone Books, Rob Sanders assembled a terrific team that in the face of imposing deadlines produced a beautiful new edition in mere months. My thanks go to Rob, and to Jennifer Gauthier, Jen Croll, Lucy Kenward, Tracy Bordian, Jessica Sullivan, Megan Jones, and Emily Cook. As always, my deepest gratitude goes to my family: my wife, Gail, and my daughters, Tara and Raina.

Further Reading

The starting point for any student of the Grand Canyon, the Colorado River, and the American West is Wallace Stegner's *Beyond the Hundredth Meridian: John Wesley Powell and the Second Opening of the West*, Houghton Mifflin, Boston, 1954. Stegner's writing is as lyrical and evocative as Powell's can be turgid and florid. Powell's original account, *Exploration of the Colorado River of the West and Its Tributaries*, published in 1875 by the Government Printing Office, appeared twenty years later as *Canyons of the Colorado*, Flood & Vincent, Meadville, PA, 1895. The contemporary edition, with an introduction by Stegner, is John Wesley Powell, *The Exploration of the Colorado River and Its Canyons*, Penguin, New York, 1987. For more on the journals and letters of Powell and his men, see John Cooley (ed.), *Exploring the Colorado River*, Northland Publishing, Flagstaff, 1987; and Michael Ghiglieri, *First Through Grand Canyon*, Puma Press, Flagstaff, 2003. For the Mormon settling of the West, see Wallace Stegner, *Mormon Country*, Duell, Sloan & Pearce, New York, 1942; and *The Gathering of Zion*, McGraw-Hill, New York, 1964.

There have been many books of photography on the Grand Canyon, all of which are readily sourced, and any number of excellent guidebooks to the river and the trails of the national park. Of particular interest as a visual chronicle is Robert Webb,

Grand Canyon, a Century of Change, University of Arizona
Press, Tucson, 1996. To sense what was sacrificed with the
construction of the Glen Canyon Dam, see Tad Nichols, *Glen
Canyon*, Museum of New Mexico Press, Santa Fe, 1999. For
a guide's-eye view of running the river, see Buzz Belknap and
Loie Belknap Evans, *Grand Canyon River Guide*, Westwater
Books, Evergreen, CO, 1989; Linda Lou Lindemann, *Colorado
River Briefs*, DeHarts Printing Services, Santa Clara, CA, 2005;
and Larry Stevens, *The Colorado River in the Grand Canyon*, Red
Lake Books, Flagstaff, 1998.

There are several fine books on the archaeology, prehistory,
and geology of the canyon, not to mention the water crisis in
the American West. For the Anasazi, see Craig Childs, *House of
Rain*, Little Brown & Co., New York, 2006; Kendrick Frazier,
People of Chaco, W.W. Norton, New York, 2005; Stephen Lekson
(ed.), *The Archaeology of Chaco Canyon*, School of American
Research Press, Santa Fe, 2006; David Roberts, *In Search of
the Old Ones*, Simon & Schuster, New York, 1996; and David
Stuart, *Anasazi America*, University of New Mexico Press,
Albuquerque, 2000. For geology, see Lon Abbott and Terri
Cook, *Hiking the Grand Canyon's Geology*, The Mountaineers
Books, Seattle, 2004; Stanley Beus and Michael Morales, *Grand
Canyon Geology*, Oxford University Press, New York, 2003;
and James Powell, *Grand Canyon*, Pi Press, New York, 2005.
For the water crisis in the American West, perhaps the best
source is Marc Reisner, *Cadillac Desert*, Viking Penguin, New
York, 1986. Also of great interest are Philip Fradkin, *A River No
More*, Knopf, New York, 1981; Heather Hansman, *Downriver:
Into the Future of Water in the West*, University of Chicago Press,
Chicago, 2019; Norris Hundley Jr., *Water and the West: The*

Colorado River Compact and the Politics of Water in the American West, University of California Press, Berkeley, 2009; Eric Kuhn and John Fleck, *Science Be Dammed: How Ignoring Inconvenient Science Drained the Colorado River*, University of Arizona Press, Tucson, 2019; David Owen, *Where the Water Goes: Life and Death Along the Colorado River*, Riverhead Books, New York, 2017; Sandra Postel, *Last Oasis*, W.W. Norton, New York, 1992; and James Lawrence Powell, *Dead Pool*, University of California Press, Berkeley, 2008.

Among the classic works of conservation are Aldo Leopold, *A Sand County Almanac*, Oxford University Press, Oxford, 1949; François Leydet, *Time and the River Flowing: Grand Canyon*, David Brower (ed.), Sierra Club and Ballantine Books, San Francisco, 1968; and Eliot Porter, *The Place No One Knew: Glen Canyon on the Colorado*, David Brower (ed.), Sierra Club and Ballantine Books, San Francisco, 1968. For wonderful portraits of David Brower and Floyd Dominy, see John McPhee, *Encounters with the Archdruid*, Farrar, Straus and Giroux, New York, 1971.

There have been surprisingly few works of literary nonfiction that take the entire saga of the canyon and its river as their theme. Among the best are Edward Dolnick, *Down the Great Unknown*, HarperCollins, New York, 2001; and Stephen Pyne, *How the Canyon Became Grand*, Viking Penguin, New York, 1998. See also Richard Fleck (ed.), *A Colorado River Reader*, University of Utah Press, Salt Lake City, 2000; Colin Fletcher, *The Man Who Walked Through Time*, Knopf, New York, 1968; Colin Fletcher, *River*, Knopf, New York, 1997; Katie Lee, *Glen Canyon Betrayed*, Fretwater Press, Flagstaff, 2006; and Ann Zwinger, *Downcanyon*, University of Arizona Press, Tucson,

1995. For an amusing, if slightly morbid, chronicle of mortality in the canyon, see Michael Ghiglieri and Thomas Myers, *Death in Grand Canyon*, Puma Press, Flagstaff, 2001.

For those keen to explore the literature at greater depth, I would recommend two sources: Helen Fairley, *Changing River: Time, Culture, and the Transformation of Landscape in the Grand Canyon*, Statistical Research, Tucson, 2003; and Earle Spamer (ed.), *Bibliography of the Grand Canyon and the Lower Colorado River from 1540*, Grand Canyon Natural History Association, Monograph #8, Grand Canyon, 1990.

And finally, no party should embark on the Colorado without at least one book by Edward Abbey. His most famous is the rollicking novel, *The Monkey Wrench Gang*, J. B. Lippincott, Philadelphia, 1975. But I actually prefer *Desert Solitaire: A Season in the Wilderness*, McGraw-Hill, New York, 1968. For a fine anthology of his writings, see John Macrae (ed.), *Edward Abbey, The Serpents of Paradise*, Henry Holt, New York, 1995.

For the unfolding water crisis that inspired the reissue of *River Notes* a decade after its initial publication, I am deeply indebted to the reporting of a remarkable cadre of journalists and commentators who kept the story alive and the nation informed, even as events moved so quickly in 2022 and the first months of 2023—notably, Bruce Babbitt, Christopher Flavelle, Natalie Koch, Nicholas Kristof, Michael Levenson, Abrahm Lustgarten, Dale Maharidge, and Fernanda Santos, writing for the *New York Times*, and Brady Dennis, Sarah Kaplan, Anumita Kaur, Joshua Partlow, and Dan Stillman, writing for the *Washington Post*.

Index

ADAM DILLON

About the Author

WADE DAVIS is currently Professor of Anthropology and the BC Leadership Chair in Cultures and Ecosystems at Risk at the University of British Columbia. From 2000 to 2013, he was a National Geographic Explorer in Residence. A photographer, filmmaker, and writer, he is the author of twenty-three books, published in twenty-two languages, including the international bestsellers *The Serpent and the Rainbow*, *One River*, *The Wayfinders*, *Into the Silence*, and *Magdalena*. He was appointed a Member of the Order of Canada in 2016 and, in 2018, was declared an Honorary Citizen of Colombia.

DAVID SUZUKI INSTITUTE

THE DAVID SUZUKI INSTITUTE is a companion organization to the David Suzuki Foundation, with a focus on promoting and publishing on important environmental issues in partnership with Greystone Books.

We invite you to support the activities of the Institute. For more information, please contact us at:

David Suzuki Institute
219 – 2211 West 4th Avenue
Vancouver, BC, Canada v6K 4s2
info@davidsuzukiinstitute.org
604-742-2899
www.davidsuzukiinstitute.org

Cheques can be made payable to The David Suzuki Institute.